STATE OF THE ART

George Eliot

STATE OF THE ART

GEORGE ELIOT

A guide through the critical maze

Graham Handley

THE BRISTOL PRESS

The Bristol Press is an imprint of
Bristol Classical Press, 226 North Street, Bedminster, Bristol BS3 1JD

© Graham Handley, 1990

ISBN 1-85399-082-5
ISBN 1-85399-083-3 pbk

A CIP catalogue record for this book is available from the British Library

Printed and bound in Great Britain by
Billing & Sons Ltd, Worcester

This book is for my good friends Perry Birnbaum

and Alan Corsbie

Contents

Acknowledgements

I particularly wish to thank my friend Dr Beryl Gray for her meticulous reading of my manuscript and her valued comments on it. I appreciate too the advice and guidance I have received from the book's editors, Michael Bird and Eleanor Porter.

Graham Handley
November 1989

Introduction

George Eliot's critical reputation stands as high now as ever before. Generally acclaimed in her lifetime, though there were dissentient voices over *Romola*, *The Spanish Gypsy* and *Daniel Deronda*, she suffered decline towards the end of the Victorian period and virtual eclipse in the first two or three decades of the 20th century. Her husband, J.W. Cross, published *George Eliot's Life: As Related in Her Letters and Journals* in 1885, some five years after her death: Gladstone, perspicacious and dry, described it as a 'reticence in 3 volumes'. Cross claimed that he had let George Eliot tell her own story by merely linking, and briefly at that, quotations from her letters and journals. But he altered, adjusted, deliberately omitted and otherwise mutilated from the best of intentions – the preservation of his wife's high moral tone – with the worst of results. The careful excision of anything damaging – some would say humanising – perpetuated the myth of a sententious, moralising and largely humourless George Eliot. In this way Cross unintentionally but undoubtedly contributed to her failing reputation.

After the publication of the *Life*, little new biographical material became available beyond the local sources in Nuneaton and Coventry. Critical studies, which often embraced biography, appeared infrequently over the next twenty years, though Leslie Stephen (1902) provides independent – and often blinkered – appraisals of the novels. The first two decades of the 20th century produced little of note, though I give some attention to Charles Gardner (1912) and Mary Deakin's much-neglected *The Early Life of George Eliot* (1913). The rash or rush of biographies incorporating critical commentary began in the 1920s and extended through to the 1940s and beyond: as I write Ina Taylor's *George Eliot: Woman of Contradictions* (1989) has just appeared. Its title underlines the continuing fascination (though in this case lamentably mishandled) that George Eliot's own story exerts, as distinct from her writings.

1

Fortunately, the pathways of scholarship and criticism have run parallel towards a deeper appreciation and understanding of the writer. The work of Gordon S. Haight, which began in the 1930s, led to the publication of the *Letters* in 1954-6 and 1978. Haight's vast knowledge of the period and of the George Eliot circles makes the edition indispensable. Moreover, Haight corrects Cross so that, in an ironic sense, George Eliot is allowed what Cross said he wanted for her, that is, to tell her own story. Haight, however, also felt the need to tell that story in explicit detail: his *George Eliot: A Biography* (1968) lays claim to being the definitive treatment. In addition to the *Letters* and extracts from the Journals, 20th-century publications of source materials such as the Notebooks, from Anna T. Kitchel's *Quarry for 'Middlemarch'* (1950) onwards, provide valuable insights into both George Eliot's range of learning and her preparations for writing. We are unlikely to discover much more about her reading, or her habits of note-taking and extract-making than is available at the moment. This even includes a catalogue of books owned by George Eliot and G.H. Lewes (ed. Baker, 1977). Beginning with Anna Kitchel's *George Lewes and George Eliot: A Review of Records* (1933), Lewes' own work and relationships, as well as his undoubted devotion to George Eliot, have been more fully documented. If current research adds to this – here I am thinking particularly of Rosemary Ashton's work – then it is true that, from the mid-20th century on, fuller exploration of the George Eliot circle has also shed new light on her and her friendships, particularly with women. Barbara Bodichon has been treated in her own right, and Edith Simcox' devotion to George Eliot, moving, poignant and possessive at every turn, has been wisely told by K.A. McKenzie (1961). It would be true to say, I think, that extracts from Edith Simcox' *Autobiography* dominate, in interest as well as space, the ninth volume of Haight's *Letters*.

Postwar critical studies of George Eliot have proliferated. These probably owe their initial impetus to F.R. Leavis' *The Great Tradition* (1948). Leavis unequivocally asserted George Eliot's primacy in English fiction, together with Jane Austen, Joseph Conrad and Henry James, with the later addition of D.H. Lawrence. This critical attention generated fresh interest in her life: the Hansons' biography (1952) registered attitudes conducive to a more sympathetic climate of appreciation. The real advance, however, was in detailed critical appreciation of George Eliot's writing. Barbara Hardy's innovative and highly influential *The Novels of George Eliot: A Study in Form* (1959) opens up the modes of tragic process and image. One chapter, 'Possibilities', evaluates with particular sensitivity and insight George Eliot's use of what is *not* said. This book anticipates Barbara Hardy's sustained and expansive investigations of George Eliot culminating in *Particularities: Readings in George Eliot* (1982).

The George Eliot critical industry has, since the early 1950s, gained a momentum which shows little sign of abating. Apart from the many articles in journals, there have been regular anthologies of criticism, including the Casebook series, the Critical Heritage series, and books such as *George Eliot and Her Readers* (Holmstrom and Lerner, eds, 1966) and Haight's *A Century of George Eliot Criticism* (1965). Individual novels, especially *Middlemarch*, have had full-length studies or groups of essays devoted to them. In particular, feminist criticism has, since the mid-1970s, given George Eliot generous attention, in terms of both textual analysis and historical placing. This has contributed to new interest in and editions of minor works, such as 'The Lifted Veil' (1985) and 'Brother Jacob' (1989; both ed. Beryl Gray), and critical studies include those by Rosemary Ashton (1983), Gillian Beer (1986) and Jennifer Uglow (1987), all of which are properly individual introductions to George Eliot's work. Here it is interesting to note that George Eliot has, regardless of the general vicissitudes of her literary reputation, consistently evoked a strong response from female (as distinct from post-1970s feminist) critics and interpreters, from Jane Carlyle in 1858 to Phyllis Rose's informed, humane and finely ironic perspective in *Parallel Lives* (1983) and beyond. The 1980 centenary of George Eliot's death sparked off a surge of activity, with the first volume of the Clarendon edition of her novels and F.B. Pinion's *A George Eliot Companion*. The birth centenary in 1919 had, by contrast, attracted scant notice.

Through Gordon Haight's initiative the texts of George Eliot's works have received detailed attention. The Clarendon edition (1980-) provides texts of the novels based on a collation of their manuscripts with editions published in George Eliot's lifetime. To date the following are available: *The Mill on the Floss* (ed. Haight, 1980); *Scenes of Clerical Life* (ed. Noble, 1985); *Daniel Deronda* (ed. Handley, 1984); *Felix Holt* (ed. Thomson, 1980); and

Middlemarch (ed. Carroll, 1986). Annotated editions of the novels and *Scenes of Clerical Life* are also available in the Penguin English Library series: here the introductory critical essays are important contributions to our understanding of George Eliot's art, in particular those by Stephen Gill (*Adam Bede*), Andrew Sanders (*Romola*), Barbara Hardy (*Daniel Deronda*) and W.J. Harvey (*Middlemarch*). *The Essays of George Eliot* (ed. Pinney, 1963) is invaluable, and is discussed in detail below.

The approach in this book is broadly chronological. It begins with contemporary reactions to George Eliot's works as they appeared, then moves through biographical, critical and scholarly responses up to the present day. The aim is not to cover every relevant piece of criticism, but I have selected writers on the basis of their critical or biographical insights, their historical typicality, or because their views contribute something of value to the debate which continues to centre on George Eliot's works. The bibliography at the end of this volume is an essential accompaniment to the summaries, references and evaluations given here. In addition, more extensive bibliographies by W.J. Harvey (1964), U.C. Knoepflmacher (1978), can be consulted, both admirably though selectively updated in *An Annotated Bibliography of George Eliot* (ed. George Levine and others, 1988). The individual reader will obviously want to add books and articles not mentioned here, and within the scope of this guide, omission does not imply rejection. Rather, it implies personal, and sometimes deliberately provocative, choice, in the hope that the reader will return to the critic and, above all, to George Eliot herself to test his or her judgments against some of the judgments recorded here.

Chapter 1
Contemporary Responses

George Eliot's first critic, Lewes apart, was her publisher John Blackwood, who issued *Scenes of Clerical Life* in his magazine, *Blackwood's* (January-October 1857). He quickly realised that his new author, Lewes' 'clerical friend', was sensitive to adverse criticism. In fact, she was so discouraged by his initial response to 'Janet's Repentance' that she abandoned her plans for a fourth 'scene', that of the 'Clerical Tutor', and began her first full-scale novel, *Adam Bede*. But *Scenes* was new in terms of presentation, treatment and emphasis. Samuel Lucas noted (*The Times*, 2 January 1858) that they offered 'clear and simple descriptions, and a combination of humour with pathos in depicting ordinary situations'. (See end of chapter for publications containing these early reviews.) *Scenes* were published in two-volume book form in January 1858. Dickens responded with immediate generosity and insight, recognising their quality. He referred to 'the exquisite truth and delicacy, both of the humour and pathos'. Significantly he added 'I have observed what seem to me to be such womanly touches in these moving fictions, that the assurance on the title-page is insufficient to satisfy me even now' (*Letters* II, 423-4). 'George Eliot' was at least partly revealed. Jane Welsh Carlyle's response was certainly enthusiastic: *Scenes* was 'a *human* book...full of tenderness and pathos without a scrap of sentimentality, of sense without dogmatism, of earnestness without twaddle – a book that makes one *feel friends*, at once and for always with the man or woman who wrote it!' (*Letters* II, 425-6). The last part of this is particularly interesting, demonstrating that, even in her earliest fiction, George Eliot's personal presence, what Edward Dowden later called the 'second self who writes her books and lives and speaks through them' (*Contemporary Review*, August 1872) was clearly apparent. The contemporary response to *Scenes* is admirably evaluated by Noble (1965) in his full-length study.

With the publication of *Adam Bede* (February 1859) George

Eliot received wider and more discriminating notice. E.S. Dallas in *The Times* was emphatic and unequivocal: 'There can be no mistake about *Adam Bede*. It is a first-rate novel, and its author takes rank at once among the masters of the art.' Dallas further defined that mastery as 'maturity of thought and feeling', 'freshness of style and warmth of emotion', as well as 'solid sense', and he offered a parallel with Thackeray, praising George Eliot's 'broad sympathy and large tolerance'. Dallas was one of her best contemporary critics. Laurence Lerner (Holmstrom and Lerner, 1966) calls him 'a pioneer in the use of psychological ideas for literary criticism, and some of his writing has a surprisingly modern ring'. Geraldine Jewsbury noted in the *Athenaeum* (26 February 1859) that *Adam Bede* was 'Full of quiet power, without exaggeration and without any strain after effect...the story is not a story, but a true account of a place and people who have really lived'. Many reviewers singled out Mrs Poyser for her proverbial coinages and earthy practicality (Dallas called her 'the gem of the novel'). There was a continuing interest in the writer 'himself' – not yet herself, since Liggins' claims to the authorship of *Scenes* and *Adam* were being advanced by Bracebridge at the time, and even supported at a distance by Mrs Gaskell.

Although *Adam Bede* was an almost unqualified success, *The Mill on the Floss* (April 1860) met with a more mixed response. Dallas, again, was forthright, though his general evaluation was qualified: 'George Eliot is as great as ever. She has produced a second novel, equal to her first in power, although not in interest.' He again noted 'the closeness of her observation, and the maturity of her thought'...'her characters speak for themselves and the dialogue is sustained with marvellous ability'. He was certain that 'The Dodson family will live for ever, and they inspire the work'. He noted the high moral conception of the novel: 'The riddle of life as it is here expounded, is more like a Greek tragedy than a modern novel' (*The Times*, 19 May 1860). The *Spectator* drew an advantageous parallel with Jane Eyre, giving Maggie the greater realism. The reviewer also noted the omnipresence of the water symbolism, and even employed the river and river-of-life imagery in his appreciation of 'this great story': *The Mill* 'is superior as a work of art' to *Adam Bede* (7 April 1860). The *Leader* (14 April 1860) posed Maggie's problem, asserting that 'a lively fancy and fertile imagination are fatal to the possessor unless accompanied by the strength of mind and moral culture necessary to hold them in subjection', and the *Guardian* (25 April 1860) concentrated on what many contemporaries regarded as a flaw in structure and emphasis. The last volume of *The Mill* was felt to be disconnected from the first two: 'There is a clear dislocation in the story, between Maggie's girlhood and Maggie's great temptation.' Admittedly, the *Leader* reviewer added 'It is perfectly true that it may be the same in real life'. The other common objection was to Maggie's obsessive passion for Stephen Guest, which was classed among 'perverted and unwholesome growths'. Later, both Swinburne (*A Note on Charlotte Brontë*, 1877) and Leslie Stephen (1902) attacked what they saw as the unnaturalness of Maggie's feelings for Stephen, whose own character was variously stigmatised. George Eliot was quick to defend her sense of truth in a letter to John Blackwood of 9 July 1860:

> The other chief point of criticism – Maggie's position towards Stephen – is too vital a part of my whole conception and purpose for me to be converted to the condemnation of it. If I am wrong there – if I did not really know what my heroine would feel and do under the circumstances in which I deliberately placed her, I ought not to have written this book at all, but quite a different book. If the ethics of art do not admit of the truthful presentation of a character essentially noble but liable to great error – then, it seems to me, the ethics of art are too narrow, and must be widened to correspond with a widening psychology (*Letters* III, 317-8).

This often-quoted passage effectively embraces George Eliot's artistic views and realistic practice: 'the ethics of art' is an important index to her own acceptance of her responsibilities – indeed her dedication – as a novelist.

Although his statement was made six years after *The Mill*, Henry James (the *Atlantic Monthly*, October 1866) concentrated on the deepening psychology of characterisation, realism and morality in the novel, exclaiming fulsomely: 'English novels abound in pictures of childhood, but I know of none more touching than the early pages of this work.' But he too was moved to point out that he found the conclusion a failure, maintaining that there was no preparation for the ending. This view was shared by others of his own time and later, but careful reading of *The Mill* cannot support it: the structural coherence and the imaginative texture reach forward almost from the first page in their insistent underlining of what is to come.

Silas Marner, that 'millet-seed of thought' sown across the intellectual planning of Romola, aroused no such clear critical divisions. Dallas (The Times, 29 April 1861), was able to indicate George Eliot's unswerving moral emphasis and her artistic integrity in some telling phrases – referring to her 'truthfulness', her concern with and for the sufferings of the poor, and the fact that she raises their 'mean existence' into 'dignity by endowing it with conscience and with kindliness'. Like other critics Dallas singles out the Rainbow Inn scene for special praise, but: 'The most remarkable combination, however, of humour with seriousness... is in the conception of Mrs Winthrop's character – a good woman who utters the most profound truths in the most confused comical fashion.' He considered the author to have 'a very spiritual nature', looking at life from 'a very lofty point of view', but added 'her novels are true novels, not sermons done into dialogue. The moral purpose which is evident in her writing is mostly an unconscious purpose. It is that sort of moral meaning which belongs to any great work of art'. The Saturday Review (13 April 1861) also noted the realistic presentation of the poor in Silas Marner, and distinguished it from Dickens' 'peculiarity' of treatment: the reviewer also sounded the comparison with Shakespeare, observing of the Rainbow Inn rustics that 'these poor people are like real poor people, just as we know that the characters in Shakespeare are like real men and women'.

Romola marked the appearance of the first positive discord in critical reception, though there was acclamation too. Anthony Trollope, whose brother Thomas Adolphus had helped facilitate George Eliot's researches in Florence, thought it her best work. R.H. Hutton, one of the few critics George Eliot herself read (and wrote to), was as definite in the Spectator (18 July 1863) as Dallas had earlier been over Adam Bede. He called Romola 'one of the greatest works of modern fiction'. He was directly concerned with the instances of Tito's character in action, asserting these to be given with a vivid particularity and consistency of presentation; for 'the same wonderful power is maintained throughout, of stamping on our imagination with the full force of a master-hand a character which seems naturally too fluent for the artist's purpose. There is not a more wonderful piece of painting in English romance than this figure of Tito'. With characteristic independence, Hutton went on to praise George Eliot's conception of Savonarola, even taking her to task for not including the martyr's supposed dying words on the scaffold ('No, not from the Church triumphant, they cannot shut me out from that'). The *Westminster Review* (October 1863) is full of general praise but bemoans the fact that *Romola* will not be popular because 'it is too great both in mind and heart'. The reviewer focused on George Eliot's 'minute analysis of moral growth', and added that 'no one has so fully seized the great truth that we can none of us escape the consequences of our conduct, that each action has not only a character of its own but also an influence on the character of the action from which there is no escape'. The historical background, however, is held to inhibit 'the human interest of the tale'. Tito, elsewhere much praised, is more of a 19th-century character in his attitudes and reactions than a 15th-century one. At the same time, there is an examination of the nature of his egoism in 19th-century terms. He is 'amiable, with great abilities and no vices (?), but living in other men's regards, and shunning every form of personal discomfort; weak, but not naturally wicked'. There is little doubt that Tito is the triumph of *Romola* for the modern reader, who sees him as one of George Eliot's continuing studies in egoism, but other voices at the time deplored this particular switch to the distant past. The *Saturday Review* (July 1863) considered that George Eliot had been 'tempted into a field... where her merits are obscured, and their effect impaired'. There is a further qualification, in fact something of a sneer: 'Nor is this instructive antiquarianism relieved by any success of historical portraiture.'

Felix Holt (June 1866) attracted a number of favourable reviews, some of which express relief at George Eliot's return to the Midland scene. In the *Saturday Review* (16 June 1866) John Morley conveyed his pleasure at being once more 'among the Midland homesteads, the hedgerows...Everybody recognises the charm of the old touch in the picture'. In fact 'charm' is a word much used of the early novels. Morley also examined the range of talk in the novel, from the miners to the shopkeepers, farmers and 'the upper servants in the butler's pantry of an old manor-house', concluding that it 'is as witty and as truthful, and in its own way as artistically admirable, as anything that the writer has ever done'. He also noted 'an enlarged compassion', and picked out one of

George Eliot's main moral and thematic concerns, here as
elsewhere; that is, to expose 'the evil usage which women receive
at the hands of men'. Felix Holt himself comes in for adverse
comment from some reviewers.

Henry James (the *Nation*, 16 August 1866) seemed, as often,
divided in his views. He referred to the way that *Felix Holt*
exemplifies 'her closely wedded talent and foibles. Her plots have
always been artificial – clumsily artificial – the conduct of her story
slow, and her style diffuse'. It is pretty damning, though the first
part of this is just, when we consider the needless intricacies of the
Bylcliffe-Transome-Trounsem legal plot which cost George Eliot
(and her legal mentor Frederic Harrison) so much labour. He also
noted something in *Felix Holt* which he was again to criticise (but
word rather differently) in *Middlemarch*, saying that there was a
'disproportion between the meagre effect of the whole and the
vigorous character of the different parts, which stamp them as the
works of a secondary thinker and an incomplete artist'. But James
too appreciated the 'broad picture' of Midland country life in an
England of thirty years past, and rightly said that 'the author writes
from a full mind'...'She has written no pages of this kind of
discursive, comprehensive, sympathetic description more
powerful or more exquisite than the introductory chapter of the
present work'. Many contemporaries agreed with him.

In the *Atlantic Monthly* in the same year (October 1866) James
reviewed his own reviews, reading again all of George Eliot's
published works. These revisions are more than interesting, since
they include much discriminating evaluation of *Adam Bede*: there
is a keen insight into Hetty, together with a determined denigration
of Mrs Poyser because she is 'too epigrammatic, her wisdom
smells of the lamp. I do not mean to say that she is not natural, and
that women of her class are not often gifted with her homely
fluency, her penetration, and her turn for forcible analogies. But
she is too sustained; her morality is too shrill'. We might agree, but
defend George Eliot in terms of her own artistic conception.

One of James' conclusions is, however, a generalisation which
cannot be ignored, as true then of George Eliot as it is now. He
observed that 'the author is in morals and aesthetics essentially a
conservative'. Another interesting comment came in the
Westminster Review (July 1866), itself a radical journal, which
pointed out that George Eliot does not explain why men become

radicals or what social circumstances in their backgrounds make them so. As Laurence Lerner (Holmstrom and Lerner, 1966) observes in his evaluation of the reviews of the novel – admittedly with the advantage of hindsight one hundred years after the publication of *Felix Holt* – George Eliot was 'a radical in opinion, a conservative in temperament, and her ambivalent attitude is perfectly reflected in *Felix Holt*'. The Victorian reticence over its 'distasteful' aspects (the *Edinburgh Review* had 'painful') led to there being little critical mention of Mrs Transome or Jermyn, the former arguably to most modern critics the outstanding psychological study in the novel.

The Spanish Gypsy was published on 26 May 1868. George Eliot's poetry, now usually regarded as lacking real poetic quality, was taken with the utmost seriousness by her contemporaries. The reviews were mixed. The themes and moral concerns were variously praised, but the standard of the poetry itself was sometimes discreetly ignored. The conflict of love and duty, a favourite one with George Eliot and given a persistent emphasis in her previous work, is here displayed at full length. James' comments strike one as pertinent here (*North American Review*, October 1868). After noting the 'extraordinary rhetorical energy and elegance' he suggests that there is 'the want of brevity, retort, interruption, rapid alternation, in the dialogue of the poem. The characters all talk, as it were, standing still'. This is just, reflecting the lack of dramatic action and the carefully-structured periods weighed down with too much thought, a deliberate elevation of perspective. The characters, James asserted, acted 'not as simple human creatures, but as downright *amateurs* of the morally graceful and picturesque'.

This accusation could hardly be levelled at *Middlemarch* when the first of its eight parts appeared in December 1871. Edith Simcox (under the pseudonym H. Lawrenny) waited until the novel was completed before producing her review (the *Academy*, 1 January 1873), which penetrates to the heart of George Eliot's artistic, moral and intellectual matter. *Middlemarch*, she wrote, 'marks an epoch in the history of fiction in so far as its incidents are taken from the inner life...as the material circumstances of the outer world are made subordinate and accessory to the artistic presentation of a definite passage of mental experience, but chiefly as giving a background of perfect realistic truth to a profoundly imaginative work'. There is some astute appraisal of character, which in its turn reflects George Eliot's own structural awareness as, for example, when she says of Lydgate that 'he appears as a masculine counterpart of Dorothea with the relative proportions of head and heart reversed'. There is praise too for the appositeness of the imagery, while George Eliot's style, 'always polished and direct, seems to have become still more sharply condensed; the dialogues, always natural, still more simple in their force'. This lacks the sophistication of the modern critical vocabulary, but Edith Simcox' evaluation certainly still rewards attention.

James, in the *Galaxy* (March 1873) somewhat reversed Edith Simcox' emphasis, but he indicated, even in terms of the imagery, his own sophistications as an emergent novelist: '*Middlemarch* is a treasure-house of details, but it is an indifferent whole...George Eliot's mind is pre-eminently contemplative and analytic, nothing is more natural than that her manner should be discursive and expansive.' He also noted 'the insubstantial character of the hero' (Ladislaw), but found some compensation in the fact that Lydgate 'is a really complete portrait of a man'. He opened up the 'treasure-house', referring to the 'superior quality' of George Eliot's imagination, and the successful effect she achieved in the lowering domestic exchanges between Rosamond and Lydgate. Of Rosamond he said 'The author's rare psychological penetration is lavished upon this veritably mulish domestic flower', the images exactly capturing the paradox of Rosamond, what she is as against what she appears to be. James himself, we feel, was gaining in stature as a critic by being exposed to the various layers of *Middlemarch*. His evaluation of George Eliot's achievement in the presentation of Casaubon conveys, in small compass, so much of her greatness: 'To depict hollow pretentiousness and mouldy egotism with so little of narrow sarcasm and so much of philosophical sympathy, is to be a rare moralist as well as a rare story-teller.' And although he cavils '*Middlemarch* is too often an echo of Messrs Darwin and Huxley' he also establishes with a bold stroke that 'George Eliot seems to us among English romancers to stand alone. Fielding approaches her, but to our mind, she surpasses Fielding. Fielding was didactic – the author of *Middlemarch* is really philosophic'.

This is high praise, but it was not a view universally shared. R.H. Hutton wrote in the *Spectator* (1 June 1872) while the Parts

were still appearing, that George Eliot is a 'melancholy teacher –
melancholy because sceptical; and her melancholy scepticism is
too apt to degenerate into scorn'. This was an unfamiliar note from
Hutton and was more than counteracted by Sidney Colvin's
detailed and sensitive notice in the *Fortnightly Review* (19 January
1873). He ranged over George Eliot's various concerns, saying
that 'The characters are admirable in their vigour and individuality,
as well as in the vividness and fullness of illustration'. How well
Colvin absorbed George Eliot's own interests and emphases is
seen in this sympathetic insight: 'there is something like a medical
habit in the writer, of examining her own creations for their
symptoms, which runs through her descriptive and narrative art
and gives it some of its peculiar manner'. Frederick Napier Broome
(*The Times*, 7 March 1873) singled out George Eliot's 'topo-
graphical power' for particular praise, which is perhaps surprising.
With the whole novel before him, Broome realised the richness of
the detail *and* the whole, remarking 'There are few novels in the
language which will repay reading over again so well as
Middlemarch'. In view of its length, this is a bold statement.

Dorothea was generally admired by the critics, some of whom
ranged from the psychological studies of Lydgate, Bulstrode and
Rosamond to the moral and social placing and effect of the Garth
family. *Middlemarch* was often felt to be weighed down by its
author's pessimism, while the unsparing realism ('distasteful'
again) was by no means universally popular. Lewes undoubtedly
followed his usual practice of keeping adverse comments from
George Eliot, but she saw enough to be able to write to Charles
Ritter (11 February 1873) 'there has not, I believe, been a really
able review of the book in our newspapers and periodicals' (*Letters*
V, 374). *Middlemarch* was to run an uneven course over the
succeeding years, the critical tendency being to elevate the early
novels at the expense of the later, more complex ones until the
middle of the 20th century and beyond.

Daniel Deronda came out in eight monthly Parts from
February to September 1876. The first review, in the *Examiner* (29
January 1876) before the publication of Book I (Books and Parts
are synonymous), drew a telling analogy with the work of a young
writer who had succeeded George Eliot as a contributor to the
Cornhill magazine: 'George Eliot's characters have not the
flexibility and variety which, for example, the author of *Far From*

the Madding Crowd, whose first chapters were mistaken for her work, succeeds in imparting to his men and women.' She was further castigated for not being able to create complex characters! R.H. Hutton (the *Spectator*, 8 April 1876) appreciated the fine irony of the exchange between Klesmer and Bult, and continued his notice in the June issue by concentrating on Daniel who, he thought, was something of a problem to George Eliot, and of course to the reader. This note was commonly sounded, but Hutton was brusquely specific when he said that the advice which Daniel gives Gwendolen on two occasions was like 'the present of a stone to one who asks for bread'. By July Hutton was praising the transcendence of the conception, referring to its having 'more of moral presentiment, more of moral providence...purposes higher and wider than that of any one generation's life'. Hutton among others praised the incisive psychological investigation and revelation of Gwendolen, but was in a minority when he also distinguished the convincing quality of the presentation of the Princess, Deronda's mother.

The *Academy* (9 September 1876) considered the novel as a whole, marking Grandcourt and Gwendolen as evidence of fine art, but finding Daniel, the minor characters and the Jewish episodes as significant weaknesses. The reviewer, George Saintsbury, felt that George Eliot was so intent on illustrating a theory that she marred the reality of her portrayals. The *Saturday Review* (16 September 1876) thought that *Daniel Deronda* showed a remarkable falling away in the author's powers, putting this down to a want of sympathy with the leading *motif* of the story, and calling it 'a religious novel without a religion'. George Eliot always felt that the Jewish parts of the novel would meet with disapproval, and they frequently did: inherent prejudice in the readership often complemented the novel's own division of interest. Blackwood, ever loyal, could praise without any thoughtful consideration the 'marvellous Mordecai'. He also had the insight to record that the 'wicked witch' Gwendolen's 'running mental reflections after each few words she has said to Grandcourt' were 'as far as I know a new device in reporting a conversation' (*Letters* VI, 182). This is a direct anticipation of Joan Bennett's critical view (1948; see ch. 7 below).

Apologists for *Daniel Deronda* were not slow in coming forward. The Jewish lobby found an articulate public voice as well as private praise in letters which greatly pleased George Eliot. In *Macmillan's Magazine* (June 1877) Joseph Jacobs undertook a spirited defence of Mordecai. Daniel, on the other hand, was seen as 'laboured', with too much space given to 'studying' rather than 'painting' him, according to R.H. Hutton, who also considered that Mirah was drawn with 'ostentatious humility'. The most original critique was Henry James' *Daniel Deronda: A Conversation* (the *Atlantic Monthly*, December 1876), which F.R. Leavis reprinted as an appendix to *The Great Tradition* (1948). James was possibly the first to identify George Eliot's unconscious humour; 'for instance, where, at the last, Deronda wipes Gwendolen's tears and Gwendolen wipes his'. Pulcheria, one of the speakers, declares that the Jewish characters 'are described and analysed to death, but we don't hear them or see them or touch them. Deronda clutches his coat-collar, Mirah crosses her feet, and Mordecai talks like the Bible, but that doesn't make real figures of them. They have no existence out of the author's study'. There are some fascinating and apposite comments: 'I never read a story with less current. It is not a river; it is a series of lakes.' We are told, rightly, that 'Gwendolen and Grandcourt are admirable' and also that 'Gwendolen is a masterpiece'. There is even time for an outrageous look back at *Middlemarch* – 'If Dorothea had married anyone after her misadventure with Casaubon, she would have married a trooper'. For James, George Eliot's use of science and scientific analogy shows that she is 'simply permeated with the highest culture of the age'. And when one of his speakers accuses her of having no sense of form, another replies that 'There is something higher than form: there is spirit'.

Edward Dowden, in the *Contemporary Review* (February 1877) considered the relationship between *Middlemarch* and *Daniel Deronda*. He asserted that in the first 'the prosaic or realistic element occupies a much larger place', and that *Daniel Deronda* was 'a counterpoise or a correlative' of *Middlemarch*. He further undertook a spirited defence of Daniel, who seemed 'happily in possession of a rich and powerful vitality'. Dowden too was happy with the scientific usage, calling it 'those accretions to language which are the special gain of the time'. He also considered *Daniel Deronda* a profoundly religious novel, but maintained that 'The Judaic element comes second in the book – the human element first'.

General appraisals of George Eliot's work followed her death, or were even undertaken as a result of reading Cross' *Life*. Thus James again (the *Atlantic Monthly*, May 1885) said that for George Eliot the novel was 'not primarily a picture of life, capable of deriving a high value from its form, but a moralised fable, the last word of a philosophy endeavouring to teach by example'. This is reinforced by 'We feel in her, always, that she proceeds from the abstract to the concrete; that her figures and situations are evolved, as the phrase is, from her moral consciousness, and are only indirectly the products of observations. They are deeply studied and elaborated, but they are not *seen* in the irresponsible plastic way'. In the *Cornhill* (February 1881) Leslie Stephen asserted that she was 'superior to all her rivals', underlining this by saying that the early works 'have the unmistakable marks of high genius'. She did for English country life 'what Scott did for the Scotch peasantry', a judgment which would certainly have pleased her. He singled out her humour and her portrayal of 'phases of religious feeling', and thought the first volume of *The Mill* registered 'the culmination of her genius'. After that there is a falling off, and *Romola* is 'a magnificent piece of cram. The masses of information have not been fused by a glowing imagination. The fuel has put out the fire'. *Middlemarch* he held to be 'rather painful'.

Trollope admired her work (*Romola*, in particular) but felt that in her later novels she was more of a philosopher than a writer of fiction. 'She lacks ease,' he concluded. Her tremendous influence was sometimes registered in an intensely personal form. Lord Acton was so moved by her death that he wrote, 'It seemed to me as if the sun had gone out. You cannot think how much I loved her'. In the *Nineteenth Century* (March 1885) he wrote 'the most interesting of George Eliot's characters is her own'. It is a neat but definitive way of emphasising the presence of the writer in her own creations. And it is this presence, I suggest, that so influenced her contemporaries in their engagement with her work. The best of her critics clearly sense that presence, not merely in the obvious convention of her use of her own voice. It was also discerned in qualities that continue to be valued: George Eliot's realism and humour, her humanity and idealism, her broad tolerance, her sense of artistic responsibility, her regional recall, particularly in the early novels, her sympathetic warmth, her religion-without-dogma based on human love. All these constitute her presence.

Lord Acton drew attention to a major thematic constant in her works: 'From the bare diagram of "Brother Jacob", to the profound and finished picture of *Middlemarch*, retribution is the constant theme and motive for her art.' This and other themes, such as the need for altruistic endeavour on behalf of others, of duty, forgiveness, dedication to work, integrity in relationships and beliefs, intelligent sympathy and moral courage, all these subserve Acton's assertion that 'The supreme purpose of her work is ethical'.

It is difficult to generalise from the selection of George Eliot's comtemporary critics included here, or indeed from the wider groupings who are not. But it will be apparent, I hope, from these quotations and references that the Victorian critics took seriously both their own art and the art they were called on to evaluate. Their approach was moral, sometimes narrowly so, but their perceptions were not blunted. What we now find natural, even essential in life, they often found distasteful. The modes of their critiques, often composed under the pressure of weekly journalism, were not those of a self-conscious academic discipline, but were directed to explore, record, evaluate and enhance. It is something of a tribute to the quality of these reviewers that they recognised excellence when they saw it; and the journals they wrote for gave them at least the luxury of space in which to set out their views. George Eliot contributed greatly to the increasing stature and status of the novel, and the serious appraisal which her contemporaries accorded her is tangible evidence of this.

Note: Students are referred to the following anthologies of criticism consulted in the writing of this chapter:

Carroll, D. (ed.), *George Eliot: The Critical Heritage* (Routledge and Kegan Paul, 1971)

Haight, G.S. (ed.), *A Century of George Eliot Criticism* (Methuen, 1966)

Holmstrom and Lerner (eds), *George Eliot and Her Readers* (Bodley Head, 1966)

Chapter 2
Reconsidered Myths

On 6 May 1880 George Eliot recorded in her Journal 'Married this day at 10.15 to John Walter Cross at St George's, Hanover Square' (*Letters* VII, 270). He was twenty years younger than she was, and the event provoked almost as much comment as her original liaison with Lewes. But she was now legally, properly, respectably a wife. The rewards were immediate, though the six months of marital intimacy remain somewhat obscured; and they have since often attracted speculative, salacious and sensationally-minded biographers with their possibilities for making fictional capital. Eleven days after the marriage her brother Isaac spoke out after a silence of twenty-three years by congratulating her. She replied with characteristic generosity – or at least without irony – 'Our long silence has never broken the affection for you which began when we were little ones' (*Letters* VII, 287). While they were on honeymoon Cross was taken ill and somehow apparently fell into the Grand Canal in Venice. The matter was hushed up, and they returned to England at the end of July. The autumn passed uneventfully, but George Eliot took a chill on 18 December and died on the 22nd. They had moved to Cheyne Walk only three weeks earlier and Cross told her devoted friend Elma Stuart, 'I am left alone in this new house we meant to be so happy in' (*Letters* VII, 351).

Five years later Cross, who lived on until 1924, had fashioned out of his loneliness a biography he regarded as suitable to George Eliot's memory. It is a biography with a difference, and one wonders if he remembered sufficiently her own expressed preference in her review of Carlyle's *Life of Sterling* (*Westminster Review*, January 1852):

> We have often wished that...when some great or good personage dies, instead of the dreary three or five-volumed compilation of letters and diary and detail, little to the purpose...we could have a real 'life' setting forth briefly and vividly the man's inward and outward struggles, aims and

achievements, so as to make clear the meaning which his experience has for his fellows.

Cross preferred, and perhaps the times demanded, a three-volume compilation, the *Life as Related in her Letters and Journals*. His own responsibility was acknowledged on the title-page: 'Arranged and Edited by Her Husband.'

His Preface, if not actually contradicting this, sets forth his aims: he tried to 'form an *Autobiography*' which shall be 'Free from the obtrusion of any mind but her own'. In transcribing the letters, for example, he declared himself to be 'keeping the order of their dates', modestly claiming some originality for his method, but adding ominously 'Each letter has been pruned of anything that seemed to me irrelevant to my purpose – of everything that I thought my wife would have wished to be omitted'. He consulted her brother Isaac about her childhood, and acknowledges the help he received from the Brays and Sara Hennell, her Coventry friends who so influenced her development. The Preface contains no mention of Edith Simcox, Elma Stuart, Barbara Bodichon, Mrs Congreve, John Chapman or Herbert Spencer, to name but a few from her London years from whom much might have been expected, but whose comments or revelations could so easily have embarassed the husband-compiler. The tone of what follows is exemplified in the penultimate paragraph: 'The size of the volumes has been determined by the desire to make this book uniform in appearance with the original editions of George Eliot's Works.' The uniformity and size go beyond measurable appearance and include the moral colour between the covers, and in this continuation of her own works the author is shown as sententious, self-conscious, and rather dull, telling her own tale primly, forsaking nature and, more disastrously, human nature, in the interests of establishing a posthumous moral security.

In the Preface to his edition of *The George Eliot Letters* (1954-78, see ch. 6 below for commentary) Gordon Haight instances some of Cross' derelictions. When George Eliot once observed that it was raining 'blue devils' Cross removed the phrase. He also cut out her description of a German performance of *Orpheus* with 'Greek shades looking like butchers in chemises', while her self-mocking look at herself 'My hair is falling off; by next April I shall be quite bald, and without money to buy a wig' (*Letters* I, xiii) was also omitted. The heaviness of Cross' editing is shown in his own statement that 'no single letter is printed entire from the beginning to the end'(*Cross* I, 38). What he did was to transpose passages from one letter to another, thus constructing his own sequence and conferring on it the moral tone and authority he required. Moreover, his dating of letters was often inaccurate, his use of the relevant calendars casual at best. It seems likely too that Cross removed the pages for 1849-54 from George Eliot's Journal, thus actively suppressing information about that vital part of her life before she left England with Lewes in July 1854. And though Haight rightly stresses that 'we should be grateful for what his pious hand has spared', he adds stringently that 'The legend of lofty seriousness, fostered in the beginning by Lewes, became through Cross' efforts so firmly fixed that it coloured her reputation as a novelist'.

After reading Cross, William Hale White, ('Mark Rutherford'), who had known George Eliot at 142 Strand, felt he had made her too 'respectable'. He added that she had not had justice done to her and that 'she has been removed from the class – the great and noble church, if I may so call it – of the Insurgents to one more genteel, but certainly not so interesting' (the *Athenaeum*, 28 November 1885). Sensitive on his wife's account, determined to perpetuate the 'respectability' of one whose early supposed lack of it had been transcended by her sybilline years, Cross certainly did an outwardly respectable job. Reader convenience is everywhere considered, with the summaries at the end of every chapter in simple note form, dates (sometimes wrong) in the margin against the letters, useful historical background details (on the Nuneaton riots which George Eliot witnessed as a child) and references to the novels or poems or essays where appropriate.

Cross never allowed the stream to get muddied; and the clear flow is sustained with little ripples of supportive commentary. There is a blandness about much of it which carries a seal of self-approval, and the small additions are always in faultless taste. Yet Cross is still for many 20th-century readers the basic source; and he has served later biographers well, providing a sequence whose omissions can be filled in either by deduction or free imagination. Even modern scholars refer to him, his closeness to George Eliot giving him a kind of authority, despite the fact that Haight's edition of *The Letters* and biography (1968) have superseded him. As I write, Timothy Hands' *A Chronology of*

George Eliot (1989) has just appeared; yet in this much-needed working accompaniment to any study of George Eliot there are as many references to sources in Cross as there are to *The Letters.* Cross did for George Eliot what Hardy did for Hardy when he dictated his own accounts of his life to his second wife, Florence; he perpetuated an image which accorded well with a self-interested hindsight and an awareness of eminence. And both in Hardy's case and George Eliot's, there has been a considerable chipping away at the image since.

Mathilde Blind's *George Eliot* (1883) pre-dates Cross by some two years. She met the Brays and Sara Hennell, carried out her own researches, and produced an informed, informative brief study which, even though dated and with some inaccuracies, reads well today. She is thoroughly acquainted with George Eliot's critical writings as well as her fiction, and feels that she would be better compared with Carlyle than with George Sand. At every opportunity she links what she knows of the life with the fictions, regarding George Eliot as the 'greatest interpreter' of English rural and provincial life. She sets out the family and Coventry influences and the complexities of Marian Evans' nature before the creative impulse transformed her into George Eliot. She praises the *Westminster Review* articles ('written in the fresh maturity of her powers'), concentrating with enjoyable particularity on 'Silly Novels by Lady Novelists'. Mathilde Blind also notes the convincing rendering of idiom and manners in *Scenes*, underlines the humour by richly selective quotations, and links *Adam Bede* to George Eliot's known theories of art, referring to her 'conscientious fidelity of observation'. She considers *The Mill* to be the most poetical of the novels, and notes in passing the incidence of death by drowning in George Eliot's fiction. There is also a finely sympathetic and thoroughly integrated analysis of Maggie's character. She then introduces readers to *Jermola the Potter* by the Polish writer J.I. Kraszewski, which pre-dates *Silas Marner* with which it has certain marked plot similarities. The main one is 'the redemption of a human soul...by means of a little child'; but she concluded that it is virtually certain that George Eliot did not know the tale. She goes on to say that the humour in *Silas Marner* is of the 'highest order', comparable to Shakespeare's. Tito (*Romola*) is acclaimed 'a unique character in fiction', while her analysis of *The Spanish Gypsy* and of George Eliot's poetry generally is brilliantly incisive. She observes of the former that, although it has George Eliot's 'instinctive insight into the primary passions of the human heart' and her 'wide sympathy', her thoughts, instead of being naturally winged with melody, seem mechanically welded into song'. But she does advocate a reading of George Eliot's poems, since they reveal 'the profound sadness of her view of life'.

Mathilde Blind's analysis of *Felix Holt* underlines the thematic constants of George Eliot's work, but she feels that this novel betrays an inferiority of execution, 'too conscious a seeking after effect'. On *Middlemarch* she reveals her uncertainty of judgment, arguing that it is 'a story without a plot', even considering that it is perhaps inappropriate to call it a novel, though her perception of characters and her analyses of them are as mature as ever. Mathilde Blind emerges as an early feminist, finding in *Middlemarch* the author's identification with 'the aspirations and clearly formulated demands of the women of the 19th century', though she admits that this identification was more with women's educational advance than with 'that other agitation which aims at securing the political enfranchisement of women'. With *Daniel Deronda* she feels, anticipating by some 60 years F.R. Leavis (1948) that there are 'two perfectly distinct narratives'. But her superb analysis of Gwendolen is imaginative, sharply-focused and sympathetic. She deplores, however, the lack of that 'rich, genial humour which seemed spontaneously to bubble up and overflow her earlier works'.

I have given Mathilde Blind space here because I feel her work merits it. Her critique is always stimulating, informed both with the specific ambience of George Eliot's works and with her own width of culture. All too often the voice of the Victorian critic is ignored or submerged by modern evaluations which have the advantage of accumulated knowledge and historical perspective, but Mathilde Blind's evaluation of George Eliot is independent and cogently argued. She is, I think, an early critic of some importance.

In 1890 Oscar Browning, who had known George Eliot in the latter years of her life and tended to stress the personal nature of her interest in him, produced a biographical-cum-critical study. He had the advantage of reading Cross, and although he found it difficult to forecast George Eliot's ultimate position, he had no doubt of Cross' contribution, praising his 'invariable account' as well as his 'reticence and good taste'. Browning's biographical sequence is followed by some critical evaluations. He stresses Lewes' influence on the plot development of *Adam Bede*, particularly his advice to George Eliot to make Dinah the principal figure of interest towards the end of the narrative. Browning also makes biographical connections: the power of *Adam Bede*, he says, 'is due to the intensity with which it represents actual life', drawn here from the relationship between Robert Evans and young Newdigate, fictionalised as Adam and Arthur Donnithorne. Although George Eliot discounted the idea that her characters were based on real people, Browning doesn't. He also points to Elizabeth Evans, the 'original' of Dinah (according to her memoral tablet) 'known to the world as "Dinah Bede" '.

The local habitation and the name of course gives George Eliot a strong regional currency, but this approach tends to militate against evaluation of the work itself. Browning does, however, formulate some independent critical ideas, including the unusual view that *Daniel Deronda* is her greatest work. It is typical of his ill-structured book that in his final section, having related George Eliot to Goethe, he should write more on the latter than the former. But for all his unevenness, the self-indulgence and lack of a coherent fame, Browning remains worth looking at, perhaps more for the stray detail than the glutinous mass. For example, 'Scientific metaphor was the best and truest instrument at her hand, and no one can deny that she wielded it with extraordinary power and success'. He quotes George Eliot on Dickens' characters 'if he could give us their psychological character, their conceptions of life, and their emotions with the same truth as their dress and manners...', and connects this with her own artistic creed and psychological characterisation. Browning's book also has an invaluable, if not always accurate, bibliography by John P. Anderson.

As early as 1880 W.E.A. Axon wrote an informative, perceptive account of a particular aspect of George Eliot's work, namely her use of dialect. He stressed both her range and her accuracy, observing that 'With the reticence of genius George Eliot obtains her effects with the slightest possible expenditure of material. She contrives to give the impression of provincial speech without importing any great number of provincial words into the text'. This was interestingly corroborated by George Eliot herself. She wrote to W.W. Skeat that her 'inclination to be as clear as I could to the rendering of dialect, both in words and spelling, was constantly checked by the artistic duty of being generally intelligible' (*Letters* IX, 39). Both Axon and George Eliot's letter to Skeat are relevant, because her 'artistic duty' involved this conscious awareness of her responsibility to her readers. About the intelligibility of her dialect she may have been over-sensitive (Thomas Noble in his 1985 edition of *Scenes of Clerical Life* notes her toning it down for the later editions in her lifetime).

Lord Acton, despite his deep love for her, registered something of the changed attitude towards her writing in his article, already cited, in the *Nineteenth Century* (March 1885). Her adherence to the ideas of Comte led her, he says, 'to analyse and to illustrate with an increasing fertility and accuracy; but she was in the clasp of the dead hand, and the leading ideas recur with constant sameness'. There is an interesting paradox here, but Acton's statement should be compared with Congreve's assertion that George Eliot 'was not a Positivist'. Ten years later, however, the rot had begun to set in. George Saintsbury (*Corrected Impressions: Essays on Victorian Writers* 1895) rejected earlier literary fashion when he said 'I never remember having read a single book of George Eliot's with genuine and whole-hearted admiration'. Her essays, he felt, were of the same standard as those of a number of 'quite second-rate authors', and he condemned Lewes' (supposed) influence by saying that 'the scientific phraseology to which he himself was more or less sincerely devoted invaded his companion's writing with a positive contagion'.

George Eliot's first serious critics, as we have seen, took rather a different view of her usage; and we might note of Saintsbury's statements that they are loose rather than carefully measured and depend for effect on generalising rhetoric rather than on the specificity of example. There is something shrill and emotive, similar to Swinburne's excitable tone in *A Note on Charlotte Brontë* (1877), when he wrote of the final volume of *The Mill* 'But who can forget the horror of inward collapse, the sickness of spiritual reaction, the reluctant incredulous rage of disenchantment and disgust, with which he came upon the thrice-unhappy third part?' This, like so many of the attacks in the years following Cross' *Life*, employs the rhetoric of a neurotic subjectivity. In 1877 Swinburne

was inflamed because the novel did not turn out as he wished: it
kept to the realities of life and not the psychology of romantic myth.
Saintsbury, eminent, widely – supposedly deeply – read in European fiction, but often dull, could say with seeming authority,
'George Eliot, though she may still be read, has more or less
passed out of contemporary critical appraisal'.

W.C. Brownell (1901), while allowing George Eliot pre-
eminence among the psychological novelists, proceeds to expose
what he considers to be her limitations. He says of her characters
that they think, 'change, deteriorate, in consequence of seeing
things differently. Their troubles are largely mental perplexities...In
George Eliot's world nothing ever happens, one is tempted to say:
certainly less, very much less, than in the world of any other writer
of fiction of the first rank'. He goes on to say that we do not
'sufficiently *feel*' with her 'personages' (the word was obviously
intended to have a distancing quality), but makes the interesting
assertion that 'Always in exteriorization George Eliot's touch
shows less zest than in examination'. Again, however, the intention
is to indicate defects in her artistic conception and practice, and
apart from the transparent inaccuracy of 'nothing ever happens'
(Hetty is responsible for her child's death, Maggie drifts with
Stephen, Baldassarre strangles Tito, Felix is charged with
manslaughter, Grandcourt drowns), there is also the kind of
criticism which itself diminishes art. Thus Brownell deplores
George Eliot's 'lack of spontaneity', the absence of which is
'particularly apparent in her style'. The implication is of course that
'spontaneity' is a desirable quality, a mark of great writing. But the
art that conceals art achieves the effect of spontaneity, and here,
for many readers, George Eliot excels. Take, for example, the
scene in *Middlemarch* where Harriet Bulstrode in terrible adversity
stands by her husband, or where, in *Felix Holt*, Jermyn seizes
Harold, turns them both to face the mirror, and asserts his
fatherhood as the fatal resemblance registers with his hitherto
unknowing son.

Brownell also says (echoing Arnold on Wordsworth) that
George Eliot 'has no style'. There follows, before the overall
limitations are re-emphasised, some evaluation of *Middlemarch*
which contains critical insights interspersed with woolly thinking.
For example, 'It is, indeed, a half dozen novels in one...it is the
microcosm of a community rather than a story concerned with a

unified plot and set of characters. And it is perhaps the writer's fullest expression of her philosophy of life'. For Brownell 'her position as a classic is doubtless assured' (though the 'doubtless' itself suggests a measure of doubt). He says that she has 'a limited imaginative faculty, a defective sense of art, and an inordinate aggrandisement of the purely intellectual in human character, which implies an imperfect sense of the completeness of human nature and the comprehensiveness of human life'. Even if we ignore the idiosyncratic use of 'aggrandisement', there is much to quarrel with. An immediate example is the 'defective sense of art': if we applied this to *Middlemarch*, the novel moderately praised by Brownell, it might suggest that the defect is in fact in the critic. He has failed to observe unity in complexity, or the running ironic appraisal, or the considered, conscious use of parallel and contrast, or to measure the effects of the interlocking imagery. Here it is strange that, in view of their emphasis on George Eliot's ethical concerns, so few critics of the late 19th and early 20th century were able to appreciate the artistic usages which implement and sustain her morality.

Brownell also comments on another important aspect of George Eliot's art, again, I think, in error. When he states that 'her intellect atones for sensuous deficiencies', it is almost as if he had never read the scenes between Arthur and Hetty, was unaware of the sexually-generated tensions between Maggie and Stephen or of the cleverly hinted intimacies and rejections between Rosamond and Lydgate. The intellect, the senses and morality are in close interacting expression in George Eliot's fiction, and she achieves what I think can be truthfully called intelligent realism; that convincing, sympathetic and complete presentation of heart and head. In the image of Gwendolen Harleth as a lily, her elasticity and freedom of movement are given a considered stress; she is sexually attractive and outwardly confident, but manifestly the same Gwendolen who creeps insecurely into her mother's bed, or who dreams that she is crossing Mont Cenis in the snow, but meets Daniel, who tells her to go back. And she is that same Gwendolen who, when she first sees Mrs Glasher, Grandcourt's mistress, feels that 'it was as if some ghastly vision had come to her in a dream and said "I am a woman's life" ' (*Daniel Deronda*, ch. 14).

Arnold Bennett had no doubt that the decline of George Eliot's reputation would continue. He wrote in his journal (13 May, 1896)

'I dipped into *Adam Bede*, and my impression that George Eliot will never be among the classical writers was made a certainty!' Henry H. Bonnell, however, found redeeming features in her novels in his *Charlotte Brontë, George Eliot and Jane Austen: Studies in Their Works* (1902). He even included the *Impressions of Theophrastus Such* in his appraisal as evidence of her many-sidedness and her particularity in the use of language. He underlined the exactitude and range of associations of her diction, picking out *sandy, pink-skinned* and *chiaroscuro*. He noted her 'happy selective ability' in words such as *greenth, calenture, pilulous* and, above all, *dynamic*, which had caused John Blackwood pleasure (and doubt) and other critics disquiet when they saw it in the first sentence of *Daniel Deronda*. Blackwood admitted that although it was as yet 'a *dictionary* word to so many people' he felt that it conveyed the exact shade of meaning she required (*Letters* VI, 183). Bonnell further illustrates George Eliot's meticulous and imaginative choice of words and images, which set up associations for the reader. When he says of *dynamic* that 'The word was seized with peculiar power at a time when electricity was revealing new possibilites of energy', he follows by suggesting that the idea is of energy which, far from being static, is in active motion. Its application to Gwendolen, who is in the (hyper)-active motion of gambling, is fully appropriate when we come to know more of her. It reflects the nervous tension of her nature.

In this brief survey of attitudes to George Eliot and her writings in the twenty or so years after her death, I have omitted one or two minor studies and a whole category of books about people and places, which constituted part of the early cottage industry of publications about her. One book stands out, I think, among these early appraisals: Leslie Stephen's *George Eliot* (1902) is of major importance. Ira Bruce Nadel, writing on 'George Eliot and her Biographers' records that Stephen's book does, among other things, place George Eliot in a European context, and that it has 'a welcomed irreverence' and is, moreover, 'an antidote to the uncritical and voluminous life Cross compiled', as well as being 'the first critical biography of Eliot and her work'.

Though not entirely accurate, this is a fair assessment of Stephen's work. His distance from his subject is apparent, and he applies his own sensible and realistic perspective. For example, he observes that 'The Warwickshire landscape is not precisely stimulating...Shakespeare had the good fortune to migrate to the centre of intellectual activity at an early period'. And so, more or less, did George Eliot; but she took with her an abundance of stimulus from her Midlands terrain, returning in identification and imagination through *Scenes*, five novels, the 'Brother and Sister' sonnets and certainly in one notable section of *Impressions of Theophrastus Such*. Stephen has a convincing intellectual grasp which gives some authority to his generalisations. For instance, he says that 'a width of sympathy was perhaps her most characteristic quality', and he also looks at George Eliot's life, if a little ironically, at least with the evidence carefully weighed. Of Lewes and George Eliot he says 'Their home became a temple of domestic worship, in which he was content to be the high priest of the presiding deity. He stood as much as possible between her and all the worries of the outside world'.

But it is when he deals with particular aspects of the novels that the quality of his criticism is apparent, though we may not agree with his emphasis or conclusion in every case. He points out (and he is *not* talking about the plots!) that George Eliot's 'situations are simple, and the effect is produced by what we can recognise as the natural development of the characters involved'. This seems to me essentially accurate, and his statement that 'The story of Hetty's wandering in search of her seducer is told with inimitable force and pathos' connects with the major strengths of *Adam Bede*; its realism, its truth to character in action, and its sympathetic immediacy. It is not merely irony which encompasses Hetty, it is compassionate irony, the 'width of sympathy' Stephen had already noted, which George Eliot particularised with such sensitivity. But when Stephen considers the ending of the novel, he notices an emphasis which subordinates such realism: 'The tragedy is put aside; all the unpleasant results are swept aside as carefully as possible, and everything is made to end happily in the good old fashion.' Well, not quite: Hetty has died on the way home, and Colonel Donnithorne is largely a broken man. But Stephen's meaning is clear (he has already indicated that he finds Dinah too good to be true), and we recall Lewes' advice that Dinah should be pushed more into the centre of the action. There *is* something of artistic incompleteness in the ending, though Stephen's generalisation remains, I think, untenable.

Stephen also finds George Eliot's conservatism apparent,

despite 'her acceptance, in the purely intellectual sphere, of radical opinions'. There are other perceptive emphases: 'Her women are – so far as a man may judge – unerringly drawn. We are convinced at every point of the insight and fidelity of the analysis; but when she draws a man, she has not the same certainty of touch.' Yet again we must qualify this generalisation. Are Lydgate, Bulstrode, Tito and Grandcourt inferior in conception and realisation to Caterina, Dinah, Romola and Mirah? Although the remark is meant as praise, it has a certain falseness: Stephen's prejudices are strong ones, as we see when he considers Stephen Guest 'a mere hairdresser's block'. He is however, happier with *Silas Marner*, describing the 'admirable passages of humour', and noting of the Rainbow Inn rustics that they show George Eliot's tracing of 'the curious mental processes which take the place of reasoning'. He stresses that 'fiction must be applied psychology', though it is clear that Stephen believes it must, in her works, be applied philosophy too. He tells us that 'she had reflected long and seriously with all her very remarkable intellectual power upon some of the greatest problems which can occupy the mind'. And Stephen, like others of his time and before, returns to the early works, where he praises the 'spontaneity' (an interesting comparison with Brownell) arising from the 'memories tinged by the old affections'. With the middle-to-late novels he is less happy. *Romola* is 'a most lamentable misapplication of first-rate powers', and is disadvantageously compared with *Silas Marner*, the bad Florentine jokes being set against the humour of the Rainbow Inn rustics, who are 'inimitable because their talk is so pointless'. These sound, integrated observations are marred by a heady rush of chauvinism, as when he states 'Tito is thoroughly and to his fingers' ends a woman,' adding 'In several of her novels George Eliot contrasts the higher feminine nature with this lower type'.

Stephen's tone and bias here are inexcusable and yet, paradoxically, he recognises Mrs Transome as the strongest, truest part of *Felix Holt*. He attacks *The Spanish Gypsy* largely because of its unlikely theme rather than the quality of its poetry: 'to throw overboard all other ties on the single ground of descent, and adopt the most preposterous schemes of the vagabonds to whom you are related, seems to be very bad morality whatever may be its affinity to positivism'. 'Armgart', he observes malic-iously, becomes 'part of the choir inaudible'. Stephen obviously registers some of the greatness of *Middlemarch* ('George Eliot's reflective powers fully ripened and manifesting singular insight into certain intricacies of motive and character'), but criticises a 'preoccupation with certain speculative doctrines'. 'Daniel Deronda is an amiable monomaniac and occasionally a very prosy moralist', and in this novel 'the characters are becoming emblems or symbols of principle, and composed of more moonshine than flesh and blood'.

Stephen's conclusions concerning *Daniel Deronda* are unequivocal. George Eliot's principal theme is 'the idealist in search of a vocation', she is in sympathy with 'a singularly wide range of motive and feeling', and she is adept at describing and revealing the conflict of motives in character. His analysis of 'the ingenious modes of self-deception in which most of us acquire considerable skill' is particularly perceptive. Finally, George Eliot has 'powers of mind and a richness of emotional nature rarely equalled'. Although Leslie Stephen's work is uneven and sometimes irrationally biased, as in the acid asides quoted above, there are, in reasonable profusion, critical insights of a rare, almost modern stamp. When he writes of George Eliot he is never dull, and although he is given to rhetorical denunciations and heavy-handed irony, he also sees into the heart of her philosophy, and sometimes into the warm heart of her feelings. Ironically, it was in the second period of general critical decline, between the 1900s and 1930s, when straightforward neglect rather than adverse criticism prevailed, that Stephen's daughter, Virginia Woolf, recussitated George Eliot's reputation with a shrewd centenary appraisal (see Woolf, [1919] 1932). Stephen cannot be neglected in the historical pattern of criticism, since his interests and sympathies were wide, and it is largely because of this that the best of his writing on George Eliot remains of interest today: the stimulus of disagreement is, after all, an important challenge to our own judgment.

Chapter 3
A Lowered Status: 1900s-1930s

The second period of critical decline, correctly called neglect by George Eliot's biographer J. Lewis May, saw little activity between Stephen (1902) and the centenary of her birth in 1919. Thereafter, there was some infrequent biographical and critical investigation of very mixed quality, up to the publication of Gordon S. Haight's *George Eliot and John Chapman* (1940).

Charles Gardner's *The Inner Life of George Eliot* (1912) has some period interest. It is also in some ways a psychobiography, though its lines are much more emotional and religious than psychological. The critical pronouncements are limited, subjective, and often untenable: Gardner believes, for instance, that George Eliot's particular strengths lie in her descriptions of 'perfect' characters, such as Dinah and Daniel Deronda.

Gardner has some interesting emphases, however. He analyses the influence of Sara Hennell, who, he says, condensed Feuerbach's beliefs into one expressive sentence: 'God is henceforth the essence of the species of humanity.' He draws attention to George Eliot's essays on Cumming (October 1855) and Young (January 1857), which reveal that 'she was still in the reaction of her revolt from Evangelicalism, and was consequently too censorious'. He believes that her article on Riehl underlines the fact that her 'view of art was part of her religious view of life'. Interestingly, Gardner says little of Lewes, except that he was anti-religious and fostered George Eliot's interest in Comte. What he does assert, however, is that George Eliot's liaison with Lewes caused her to be beset by guilt 'till Death removed her companion, and put an end to her lawlessness'. When he comes to the fiction, Gardner registers some established responses, for instance the fact that 'Janet's Repentance' is inferior to the first two clerical scenes, with Janet being the major blemish in her own story, since, whatever her faults, he feels that she 'never took to drink'. George Eliot's presentation of her religious characters is her 'supreme achievement', and Gardner's reading of *Romola* leads him to an easy biographical identification, for here 'George Eliot gave utterance to her inmost thought of her own act of rebellion'. There is some reasonable analysis of the poetry, with the theme of 'The Choir Invisible' ('Man's immortality is in his after-effects') reflecting her religious concerns. But *Daniel Deronda* is her 'supreme achievement' (yes, he repeats the phrase), demonstrating her wide and prophetic religious affiliations, for she had discovered that Judaism, like Gwendolen's glance, was 'dynamic'. Gardner's study is often dated and self-indulgent, though his occasional flashes of insight can still be rewarding.

Mary Deakin's *The Early Life of George Eliot* (1913) is different in kind and quality, though interestingly, but much more effectively, it singles out the essays treated by Gardner for rigorous scrutiny. Few later writers on George Eliot acknowledge their debt to Mary Deakin, whose study covers her career up to the publication of *Adam Bede.* The approach is scholarly, a refreshment of facts without speculative sensations. Mary Deakin quotes Scherer on Cross' *Life*: 'In these three volumes we must look rather for the materials of a book still to be written than for the book itself.' These are wise words, and Mary Deakin writes one of the books to be written with selective attention, sound critical discipline and considerable imagination. Preparing for close scrutiny of the essays, she says that George Eliot's contributions to the *Westminster Review* and the *Leader* have not received due attention in terms of their importance in her development, and she also turns to the 'Brother and Sister' sonnets of 1869 (anticipating Ruby Redinger, 1975). Her comments and evaluations are worth reviewing here because their essential rightness is, I think, unassailable, despite the discoveries which have marked George Eliot scholarship since. Mary Deakin identifies the sonnets as 'the only bit of pure autobiography we possess till we come to her letters'. At the age of fifty George Eliot wrote the poems with a nostalgic tenderness and loving identification with her childhood days and her brother Isaac. There are ambiguities within them – all is not idyllic – but Mary Deakin is right to accord them importance.

This early period of George Eliot's life is subjected to a sympathetic examination, modest and accurate in its emphases: 'The remembrance of those years was always there with its restful, refreshing power, a priceless possession for a nature given to great intellectual effort and strong emotion.' Her informed analysis of the influence of Strauss and Charles Christian Hennell on George Eliot, then Marian Evans, is succinct, clear, beyond contradiction. She believes that although Marian Evans admired Strauss, she was partly in conflict with him. She did not like the absence of a spirit of worship in him, nor could she accept 'the absolute exclusion of the passion of sympathy'. She preferred Charles Hennell, though he was not as great a scholar as Strauss, because he was of a more religious nature; 'understood better the need of mankind in general for something to worship'. After commenting on the well-known fatigue and strain that Marian felt after completing her translation of Strauss, Mary Deakin adds that she had received 'a valuable training in knowledge of the capabilities of the English language'.

There is always method in Mary Deakin's approach. She quotes from a letter not published in Cross in which the twenty-five-year-old Marian Evans writes 'What should you say to my becoming a wife?...I did meditate an engagement...'. She gives the date as 1 April 1845, though Haight (*Letters* I, 188) prints 21 April, and this interesting inclusion is further evidence of Miss Deakin's careful covering of the ground. She traces, as indeed Gardner had just traced, Marian's specific debts to Richardson and Rousseau. She emphasises the way she assimilated what she read, observing that as she matured 'she had learnt the highest use of reading...A book was now a power in her life, not so much because it taught her something as because it made her the more able to teach herself'.

Mary Deakin rates the Coventry period in Marian's development very highly, saying that it was of greater importance than her time in London in her coming to understand 'the mysteries of humanity'. With the London period she deals critically, noting that in Marian's review of Mackay's *Progress of the Intellect* (January 1851) her 'style has much of the dignity we find in the early novels, something, too, of the grace, but little of the beauty and resonance: it is not yet quickened by the fine, almost imperceptible vibrations of strong, warm feeling.' It is this kind of sensitive comment, based on a thorough familiarity with Marian Evans/George Eliot's work, which distinguishes her criticism. She indicates carefully the attractions of Feuerbach for Marian and examines her *Westminster Review* contributions during 1851-7. She maintains that these show another side of the writer, one where she is 'judge and critic, laying bare impostures, inconsistencies, shams, and hypocrisies with unsparing justice'. There is 'glowing indignation, biting satire...fearless denunciation'. Although Mary Deakin's images may be somewhat strained, we know when we have read some of the essays exactly what she means: 'Into the temple of humanity she enters as a daring reformer, unceremoniously overturning the table at which Cumming changed money and the seat where Young sat selling doves.' The essays establish Marian Evans/ George Eliot's integrity, for 'She cannot let a falsity pass, whether in ethics or art'.

Mary Deakin establishes her own critical perspective on George Eliot's early fiction by referring to the 'skilful and harmonious blending of the objective and the subjective'. This is further defined by a stress on the objective quality of *Silas Marner* and the predominance of the subjective in *The Mill,* and it seems to accord with George Eliot's own statement that she at first conceived *Silas Marner* as lending itself to metrical treatment. Connectives between the essays and the fiction are now stressed. Thus of the article on Cumming ('The opening is almost as powerful and bitter as Swift') she says that 'one cannot but think of the sympathetic treatment of Evangelicalism in "Janet's Repentance", and we have a momentary feeling of wonder when we look at the two side by side and remember that less than two years divide them'. Wonder we may, but the fact is that 'Janet's Repentance' is an early revelation of George Eliot's broad tolerance: it is not the religion but the nature of the religious man or woman which concerns her.

The analysis of the essay on Riehl (July 1856) is finely done, tracing the connections with George Eliot's later fictional practice. Her evaluation of *Scenes* is mature, and anticipates much of the emphasis to be found in later criticism. First, she notes the accomplished use of dialogue, George Eliot's difference from other writers being crudely but effectively put: 'It is just in the dialogue parts where most writers use the higher power of the literary language, that she uses the lowest.' This is effectively saying that her people talk like real people, rather than like characters in books. Janet is given special praise, for she is the first of a line of female characters including Maggie Tulliver and Dorothea Brooke 'who have a startling power of life in them'. She feels, and some would agree with her, that there are characters 'whom we seem to know better than our own sisters – better, even, than ourselves'. Mary Deakin qualifies her appreciation of 'Janet's Repentance', stating that George Eliot's satire 'has not enough rapidity and lightness', but her overall summary of *Scenes* is so good that I give it here in full. *Scenes*, for her, embodies all George Eliot's greatness:

> All the deep, warm sympathy with human suffering; the insistent effort to rouse interest in the ordinary people and things about us; the understanding treatment of human nature in many varied phases; the high yet sane ethical tone; the recognition of the laws that govern us as absolutely as other laws govern the rocks and stones and trees; the tender humour, bright wit, and exquisite pathos; the closeness to life as we all know it, and the avoidance of the fantastical or bewildering – these qualities which are found in all her books are found in the first.

Mary Deakin's contribution to George Eliot studies, though limited in scope, is not inhibited either by Cross or by the critical climate of the early 20th century. Even so, in three important biographies of George Eliot by Blanche Colton Williams (1936), Gordon Haight (1968) and Ruby Redinger (1975), Mary Deakin does not appear in the index; a sad, if innocent omission. The intelligent spadework she did after Cross through deduction and discovery, her measured investigation of the name and nature of the influences on Marian Evans' religious and intellectual development, her linking of life and art, her independent and striking analysis of the *Westminster Review* essays, her ability to connect that work with the early fiction, and her evaluation of that fiction – all these make Mary Deakin's work highly important. Those later critics who revived George Eliot's reputation often unwittingly endorsed her evaluation.

The centenary of George Eliot's birth in 1919 gave rise to one article of outstanding importance, Virginia Woolf's tribute in the *Times Literary Supplement* of November 1919. She notes at once what has become a commonplace of 20th-century criticism; that George Eliot's writings arose from the new freedom which her liaison with Lewes gave her. She boldly describes those works as a 'plentiful feast'. But since the outward circumstances of her life with Lewes made for constriction because of the unconventional, supposedly immoral nature of her behaviour, she turned 'her mind to the past, to the country village, to the quiet and beauty and simplicity of childish memories and away from herself and the present'. Virginia Woolf finds 'light and sunshine' in *Scenes*, where they might seem rather sombre (consider Milly's death, Amos' desolation and enforced move, Mr Gilfil's brief marriage, Tryan's death and Dempster's savagery). She generalises lyrically, observing 'The flood of memory and humour which she pours so spontaneously into one figure, one scene after another, until the whole fabric of ancient rural England is revived, has so much in common with a natural process that it leaves us with little consciousness that there is anything to criticise'. Of course there is much to criticise, but by 1919 literary criticism was not yet expected to demonstrate through particularities, the specifics of close analysis, that a generalisation could be solidly, certainly ventured. Even so, Virginia Woolf picks out some important aspects of George Eliot's concern in the early works, for example the fact that she can make us share the lives of her Midland people, 'not in a spirit of condescension or curiosity, but in a spirit of sympathy'. The stress is on the associations of the past imbued with an ever-present humanity. She praises the humour of the novels and their social range, adding 'Over them all broods a certain romance, the only romance that George Eliot allows herself – the romance of the past'.

That past in George Eliot is of supreme value, but Virginia Woolf sees it as only a part of her 'true flavour'. She places *Middlemarch* firmly where criticism following Leavis (1948) has generally placed it, at the head of George Eliot's works: 'It is not that her power diminishes, for, to our thinking, it is at its height in the mature *Middlemarch*, the magnificent book which with all its imperfections is one of the few English novels written for grown-up people.' We note the patrician tone and perhaps ponder 'all its imperfections' (are there that many?), but the statement is grandly clear in its emphasis.

The centenary 'tribute' then takes the form of critical censure, or at least is qualified by it. As Leslie Stephen (1902) had done, she asserts George Eliot's 'inability to draw the portrait of a man', then questions her dialogue, an aspect of her art which would probably today be regarded as a particular strength: 'It is partly that her hold upon dialogue, when it is not dialect, is slack, and partly that she seems to shrink with an elderly dread of fatigue from the effort of emotional concentration.' The reverse is surely the case, and the power of dialogue and the 'emotional concentration' increase in intensity and effect in the last two novels (there is no 'elderly fatigue' in either). I am thinking especially of dialogue in the scenes of domestic suffering between Lydgate and Rosamond, Dorothea and Casaubon in their respective trials and the conscious intimate adversity in which they find themselves; the anguished, ironic exchanges between Rex Gascoigne and his obdurate father; Klesmer in interaction with Bult, or, more movingly, in the proposal scene with Catherine Arrowpoint; or Gwendolen with Grandcourt. To be fair, Virginia Woolf discerns the developing artist in George Eliot, admitting that 'if we confine George Eliot to the agricultural world of her "remotest past" ' we 'diminish her true greatness'. It is a graceful admission, but although there seems to be a general admiration for her subject, there is also some unease in admitting it. Her final identification is of the author with her creations – 'the struggle ends, for her heroines, in tragedy or in a compromise that is even more melancholy. But their story is the incomplete version of the story of George Eliot herself'.

Oliver Elton in *A Survey of English Literature 1830-80*, (1920) quotes R.H. Hutton's discriminating statement that George Eliot could 'see and explain the relation of the broadest and commonest life to the deepest springs of philosophy and religion'. Elton, though he stresses what he sees as George Eliot's deficiencies (for example 'that while exhaustively describing life she is apt to miss the spirit of life itself') has the major merit of going to the text itself and not just trying to produce an effect by unsubstantiated generalisations. Yet his emphases are odd. He considers Casaubon and Bulstrode to be the 'least real' of her characters, though he uses the critical cliché of his own and later times in defining Ladislaw as 'mere pasteboard'. For Elton *Middlemarch* is 'almost one of the great novels of the language', but he deplores its lack of 'ease and play and simplicity', and wishes that there could have been 'a little less of the anxious idealism which ends in going beyond nature'. He acknowledges George Eliot's strengths, however, ('a lawyer's grasp of the facts and a psychologist's vision of the motives'). She makes a good 'carpentry of the plot', and he registers the quality of her realism without mentioning the word, instancing Mr Tulliver's swearing on the Bible as an index to this.

George Eliot records the 'ferocity' and the 'pathos of dull and puzzled minds'. Elton is often overlooked and also condemned, for example by Leavis in *The Great Tradition* (pp. 145-6), but his comments can be perceptive and rewarding: 'Her tolerant understanding sympathy with common people is a source of her power and her humour. It is seen at its purest in the talk of Adam Bede's mother, or of the drinkers in the Rainbow at Raveloe.'

Elton also believes that she is 'melancholy because of her painful, uneasy turn for analysis, because she hears what she calls, in a noted phrase, "the roar that lies on the other side of silence"'. Better still are George Eliot's revelations of the 'minute, unspoken play of motive that lies behind an ordinary conversation'. This leads Elton to the Grandcourt – Gwendolen dialogue in chapter 11 of *Daniel Deronda*, though, unlike John Blackwood earlier or Joan Bennett later, he is not impressed. He sees it as a falsification or distortion, and uses one of George Eliot's own scientific analogies: 'we feel instinctively that there is something wrong with the method, and not merely with the style. If you apply to life a microscope of too high a power, you will see life wrong'. There is something wrong with the analogy, and perhaps the science: one is tempted to say that George Eliot employs an expanding lens. In any case, the important thing is that she sees the inward life right.

Elton does focus on aspects of her art, and like so many critics he stresses her moral concerns, the 'ethical habit of her mind' which leads her to a full representation of the theme of retribution. He refers generously to 'the untramelled sense of beauty' found in such abundance in *The Mill,* and he notes George Eliot's fondness for confessional scenes, instancing the interview in prison between Dinah and Hetty, where 'the dialect is evangelical'. He considers other similar scenes of a secular nature, such as those between Felix and Esther, or Dorothea and Rosamond, finding them 'none the less impressive'. To this could be added the scenes between Maggie and Dr Kenn, or Maggie and Philip, and above all, those between Daniel and Gwendolen.

This chapter on George Eliot's period of lowered critical status concludes with a book published some fifteen years after Elton's, David Cecil's *Early Victorian Novelists* (1935). It remains fashionable to denigrate Cecil in comparison with Leavis, and to regard his evaluation of George Eliot as bigoted and limited. But there is some sound, reasoned criticism in his section on her, and, when he resists the temptation of rhetoric and writes with the text in view, his work can be illuminating. He develops the established theory that George Eliot's ideas, those with which she invests her characters, are exclusively moral, and that the sufferings and inner conflicts her characters endure 'are always moral conflicts'. This is the enduring mainstream of George Eliot criticism. But when we reach such exemplary egoists as Rosamond Vincy and Grandcourt we might argue that Cecil's 'exclusive' definition hardly applies, that it could not do justice to the impenetrable nature of these characters. Cecil in fact qualifies it: apparently it is only her 'serious' characters who 'are envisaged exclusively in their moral aspect. They are portraits of the inner man, but portraits not designed like Charlotte Brontë's to exhibit the colour of his temperament, but the principles of his conduct – his besetting sin, his presiding virtue'. Even so, the definition is limiting, as if George Eliot were concerned merely with one dominant trait rather than the reality of 'conflicting' ideas, paradoxes within characters, contradictions within temperament.

Cecil places deliberate stress on George Eliot's intellect, which he describes as the source of her success. In relation to her artistic awareness, wisdom and philosophy this seems justified, but her humanity is arguably just as important, if not more so. He details her intellectual analysis of character, noting her ability to distinguish between, then integrate, its various elements. Here he provides a more original insight: 'It is this grasp of psychological essentials which gives her characters their reality,' and in this particular aspect of her art she is like no other Victorian novelist and in fact goes far beyond them. This is because 'her characters, unlike theirs, are always consistent...they are always true to themselves...It gives her the power which won her the admiration of Proust, the power to describe successfully how a character develops'. This mastery of psychological essentials enables her to draw complex characters, who, Cecil asserts, 'always hang together, are of a piece, their defects are the defects of their virtues'. Since she possesses this sharp, clear insight, her male characters are, in fact, often successfully conceived, though he would except Ladislaw; 'a schoolgirl's dream, and a vulgar dream at that'. However, while most agree that Ladislaw is not one of George Eliot's most fully achieved characters, 'vulgar' is a judgment that in this case tells us more about the critic than his subject.

There are curious contradictions in Cecil's essay. On the one hand he could write – 24 years before Barbara Hardy changed the face and the direction of George Eliot criticism with her study of form (1959) – 'With her greater consistency goes a greater command of form'. Her sense of structure 'is the very substance of her primary conception' and 'All is co-ordinated, all is proportion, all is tidy'. And with this goes comparison with great European novelists, for she is 'the only novelist of her time...who holds the same conception of her art which is held today'. On the other hand, he could assert that 'An exclusively moral point of view is, at any time, a bleak and unsatisfying affair'. Note the vagueness of the last word, and the failure to include tolerance, sympathy, understanding and humour, all central to George Eliot's ethical presentation. Moreover, her virtues 'are negative sort of virtues', and here he cites as evidence the Finale of *Middlemarch*, where George Eliot 'anxiously tries to convince us that Dorothea's unselfish devotion to husband and children made up for her failure to realise her youthful dreams. But she does not even convince herself. Do what she will, she cannot disguise the fact that the thought of Dorothea's life leaves her disappointed, disheartened and depressed'. This failure to respond to George Eliot's intentions, or indeed to read at all closely, is inexcusable, and in the full context of her story, Dorothea's final restriction to a domestic sphere of influence is a trenchantly ironic comment on the woman's lot (both in Dorothea's time and in George Eliot's own), not evidence that George Eliot was trying to avoid her own conclusions. She has no need to try to convince herself or us of what happens to Dorothea: she is too aware of the many and varied pressures in relationships and communities to wish to avoid the truth.

Cecil also accuses George Eliot of being a Philistine, of 'paying lip-service to art', though in fact George Eliot's abiding interest in art in general and her own art in particular is apparent from her essays onwards, and a glance at some of the pronouncements in her letters reveals the high seriousness of her dedication to the novel and indeed to a broadly-based culture. From here Cecil proceeds to attack as inadequate her 'criticism' of life. He then draws his famous analogy with Tolstoy: 'Compared to Tolstoy's it seems petty, drab. *Middlemarch* may be the nearest English

equivalent to *War and Peace*, but it is a provincial *War and Peace*.'
The comparison, though it sounds well, is as ridiculous as
comparing the topography of Russia with that of England. After
this Cecil turns George Eliot's sense of form against her. I quote
fully here, since the wording of the appraisal reveals its limitations:

> Life is chaotic, art is orderly. The novelist's problem is to evolve
> an orderly composition which is also a convincing picture of
> life. [Jane Austen, he observes, solves this problem
> completely.] George Eliot does not. She sacrifices life to art.
> Her plots seem too neat and symmetrical to be true. We do
> not feel them to have grown naturally from their situation like
> a flower, but to have been put together deliberately and
> calculatedly like a building. For in spite of her determination
> that her story should develop logically, she has not that highest
> formal faculty which makes development appear inevitable,
> she has to twist facts to make them fit her purpose.

This is a curious attitude; one of the tasks of the novelist is, after
all, to use (not twist) facts so as to both support and defy logic,
since the likely and the unlikely coexist so closely in character and
in life. This is why we accept, for example, Dinah's renunciation of
her mission when she finds herself in the unlikely situation of being
in love with Adam. All George Eliot's novels in fact demonstrate
the natural inevitability of consequences, of change, of discovery
and self-discovery.

Cecil considers that George Eliot imposes a moral law on her
characters. He cites Godfrey Cass as an example, but takes no
account of Godfrey's resenting his childlessness because of
Nancy, or because of his guilt at constantly seeing Eppie, or from
the simple egoistic wish to make amends and by so doing be
thought well of. It is not 'a gratuitous piece of poetic justice
imposed on him by the arbitrary will of his creator'. It is simply that
Godfrey's maturity is undermined by the same egoistic blindness
to the needs of others which characterised his irresponsibe young
manhood. Despite his guilt, he is shown to be unaware of his wife's
integrity. The moral flaw is inherent, not imposed. Godfrey remains
a remarkable study, part of the realistic core at the heart of the
fable. A comparison with Dickens follows, George Eliot being
inferior to him 'in creative imagination', something we can accept
since her realistic psychological integration of character is often
much greater than his. But Cecil will not relinquish the analogy,

developing the observation that her imaginative recreation of Warwickshire is less powerful than Dickens' re-creation of London: 'George Eliot's Warwickshire shows a little devitalized – not a first-hand painting but a careful coloured engraving.' Again I doubt the value of the analogy itself – a more telling one might have been made with Emily Brontë – but in any case Cecil's aural and auditory responses seem inadequate. And it is extraordinary to describe Maggie and Dorothea as 'bodies laid out in the dissecting-room, not moving flesh-and-blood human beings,' arguing that they never get free of their creator, that they do not have independent lives. This leads to the well-known 'there was something second-rate in the essential quality of George Eliot's inspiration': her imagination was weighted down 'with a great load of analytic comment'.

In his final highly rhetorical analysis Cecil calls her the heir of Dickens and Thackeray, the forerunner of Hardy and James: 'She stands at the gateway between the old novel and the new, a massive caryatid, heavy of countenance, uneasy of attitude; but noble, monumental, profoundly impressive.' This descriptive generalisation condemns through innuendo and the de-humanising though resonant associations of the weighted words (which recall certain famous descriptions of George Eliot's own features). How far all this is from her treatment of Maggie's anguish, or Dorothea's or Gwendolen's, or the suffering of that unique sinner Mrs Transome. How far from such creations as Mrs Poyser, the Dodson aunts, Mr Brooke or Mrs Cadwallader. And how far from her mature rendering of male psychology in Lydgate or Bulstrode or the silent corrosions of Grandcourt. Yet Cecil remains important, whether we admit agreement or maintain dissent (to appropriate Deronda's words in ch. 18). He provides some acute insights and judgments, though he too easily falls into the accepted denigrations of his time.

Chapter 4
Towards Revaluation

Until the 1940s it is generally difficult to separate biography and criticism. In the previous chapter I included straight-forward literary appraisal with studies combining biography and criticism, though with a bias towards either scholarly or critical interpretation. Here I consider a number of general studies or introductions to George Eliot, together with Anna T. Kitchel's pioneering work, today often overlooked, *George Eliot and George Lewes: A Review of Records* (1933), although it concentrates largely on Lewes, the partner who made so much of her work possible. The other studies, with the possible exception of Blanche Colton Williams' *George Eliot: A Biography* (1936), fit into the mixed category indicated above. They all reflect the concerns of their time and, again with the exception of Kitchel and Williams, are not by writers dedicated to the study of George Eliot. That kind of specialisation is more characteristic of the postwar period and beyond.

Elizabeth Haldane's *George Eliot and Her Times* (1927) is interesting for its particular perspective and its overall lack of method. She takes the view from the start that Cross' *Life* will never be superseded, and that George Eliot's appeal lies largely in those 'early books' which describe country life in the Midlands. She quickly produces such unsubstantiated statements as 'George Eliot, with all her passion for tradition, was one of the greatest rebels'. She singles out the essay on Heine (January 1856) for special mention: 'As criticism the article is admirable, and it has just that sympathetic touch as regards the man and his terribly suffering life, and even his occasional lapses into coarseness, that makes it specially valuable.' And she abstracts from 'Silly Novels by Lady Novelists' the important statement: 'Art is the nearest thing to life; it is a mode of amplifying experience and extending our contact with our fellow-men beyond the bounds of our personal lot. All the more sacred is the task of the artist when he undertakes to paint the life of the people.'

For Elizabeth Haldane, the strengths of the early works derive from the fact that George Eliot did not as yet moralise or 'paint the lily with the reflections of the philosopher', though this seems a dubious judgment. She has, however, the merit of questioning George Eliot's artistic sense in *Scenes*: she is uncertain about the epilogue in 'The Sad Fortunes', though she considers Milly's death is unsurpassed in its beauty and simplicity. On *Adam Bede* she notes 'Perhaps the author does not touch the lowest strata of rural life, like Hardy'. She calls *The Mill* 'a woman's autobiography' and interestingly remarks that Stephen Guest is 'not intended to be an attractive character'. Her observation of George Eliot's use of mottoes, which can 'savour of that kind of ethical rhetoric masked by rather pompous imagery which characterises her acknowledged poetry', is apt and ahead of its time in critical focus. But the book fades away feebly.

J. Lewis May (1930) asserts that George Eliot stands supreme for her pictures of 'a vanished England, of England in the days before the coming of the railroad and the electric telegraph'. Interestingly May harks back to Dowden (1877) when he observes that 'the abiding influence...resides in the personality we may discern behind the writing'. *Adam Bede* and *The Mill* are her triumphs (they 'are great commentaries on human life'), but 'the one flawless thing George Eliot ever wrote' is 'Mr Gilfil's Love-story', even considering that this follows 'Amos Barton', where 'the grandiloquence is frequent and terrible'. 'Janet's Repentance' is second-rate. These judgments virtually place May among the descriptive and generalising critics, yet he sometimes penetrates his own layers of woolly thinking and arrives at a stimulating conclusion: 'she is in fact, whatever her theories may have been, an intensely religious writer. The whole effect of her work is to emphasise and magnify those beliefs which, intellectually speaking, she had discarded long since. Intellectually, her reactions to the spirit of the age led her to embrace its scepticism.' This is an admirable summary, but when May considers other works we see just how he reflects the spirit of his age. *Silas Marner* is 'too sentimentally idyllic' and is only 'saved by its humour', and *Daniel Deronda*, with which critics ever since its contemporary reviewers have had difficulty, is 'a painful example of gifts misapplied and overloaded with futile theories'. In the preceding chapter we noted Cecil's preference for Jane

Austen. May had anticipated him here, but with a different emphasis: 'As an artist, Jane Austen is incomparably superior to George Eliot: as an interpreter of human life, as a reader of the human heart, she is immeasurably her inferior.'

Anne Fremantle (1933) provides a neat if subjective introduction: this biographer has actually discovered something sensational which can be documented, for she indicates the nature of the relationship between George Eliot and John Chapman, which Haight was to develop at book-length a few years later. She has little time for George Eliot's essays, and her subjectivity appears in such assertions as that we must all have somewhere for refuge, 'And Marian Evans' secret garden was the lost paradise of Griff'. To be fair, Anne Fremantle's style is not generally so cloying, and much of her study is fresh, warm and imaginative. She says of *Adam Bede* that 'It is christened not with holy water but the blessed earth', and of *The Mill* 'It is her own Odyssey whose Ithaca is always behind and not before'. She reinforces this, quoting Proust's admission that 'Two pages of *The Mill* can bring tears to my eyes'. She alternates between the bluntly outspoken – George Eliot returned 'to her old vomit, positivism' and the poetic – *Silas Marner* is 'the exquisite Benjamin of the Warwickshire idylls'. She can even combine sentiment and irony: 'It was the last rose of summer – *Romola* already has a Michaelmas air.' She pulls no critical punches: the character Romola is 'merely laughable', Felix Holt's 'Address to Working Men' is 'singularly inept', while *The Spanish Gypsy* is 'laboured and heavy, a badly made fake of real poetry'. *Middlemarch* is 'the sublimation, the idealisation of George Eliot's Coventry days'. It is of course much more than that. Anne Fremantle has some independent insights but little discipline in her approach, and she is ultimately of her time in regarding George Eliot as weighed down by intellect, and in embracing the then commonly-held view that 'Her attempt to carry ethical purpose and erudition into her art nearly destroyed that art'.

I make no apology for including Anna Kitchel's *George Lewes and George Eliot: A Review of Records* (1933), despite the fact that much of what she says is now common currency. Her pioneering book not only establishes Lewes in his own right (and write) but underlines the mutual dependence he and George Eliot felt in their relationship. Anna Kitchel makes biographical speculation irrelevant. She goes to the sources. The first part of her study is concerned with Lewes and has some bearing here in terms, for example, of Lewes' influence in making the teachings of Comte more widely known in Britain (and more specifically known to Marian Evans). She says of Lewes' *Biographical History of Philosophy* that it contains an 'insistence on clarity above all things', and she also draws attention to Lewes' novel fragment *The Apprenticeship of Life*, written in the manner of Goethe's *Wilhelm Meister*. This contains a character, Hortense, who is a 'St Simonian, and believes that *love is the only bond of marriage*'. The italics are Anna Kitchel's: the importance for the future George Eliot is evident, for the phrase defines a tenet of Feuerbach's with which she was in complete sympathy.

Lewes' commitment to the *Leader* is given a considered evaluation, and again it is clear that some of its humanitarian concerns, such as 'the right of every one of our fellow citizens to live by work' may have influenced George Eliot. Certainly she would have appreciated Lewes' outspoken 'We want a new church because the Church of England is dead, for it stands immovable upon tradition and formulas', though her own tolerance and respect for tradition could not possibly have admitted this extreme view. The *Leader* was 'deeply concerned with scientific progress'; it attacked clairvoyance and spiritualism, discussed Dickens' use of spontaneous combustion in *Bleak House* and exposed poor novels. Anna Kitchel is, like all writers on George Eliot of her time, heavily dependent on Cross, but she is aware of its 'too well expurgated pages'. She mentions both Anne Fremantle and Chapman's diary and its importance, and she sees Lewes' advocacy of Comte influencing George Eliot, who reflected: 'My gratitude increases continually for the illumination Comte has contributed to my life.' She says that *The Spanish Gypsy* is steeped in Comte, with its ideas of 'race' and 'social duty' in Fedalma's story, and adds that Lewes expressed his 'delight' in the poem. Her study is a fascinating introduction to the influence Lewes exerted on George Eliot. That influence, it must be allowed, sometimes resulted in activities on her part which were not necessarily right in terms of judgments or imagination, but this cannot detract from the man and his own vibrant and wide intellectual spectrum: without Lewes there would have been no George Eliot.

The most important full-length study between Cross (1885)

and Haight (1968) is undoubtedly that of Blanche Colton Williams (1936). She has, in fact, plenty to say about the fiction and the poetry, and although the book is not an integrated life-into-art study, it goes some way towards being so. She reminds us that in 1901 Frederic Harrison said 'It will be the duty of the most serious criticism of another generation to revive the reputation of George Eliot as an abiding literary force'. Blanche Williams proceeds to do this, and some of her statements are bold indeed when set against other valuations of her time: 'In representing life and the way life works, George Eliot is above Dickens; in definitely localised setting, she is more nearly universal than Thackeray...in modernity of thought and feeling she is with Meredith and Hardy.' But, like her contemporaries, Blanche Williams indulges the subjective as well as the critically independent, so that she can praise 'the nostalgia of genius' which captured her childhood home and the Warwickshire countryside in her works, while asserting that her brother Isaac's being given a pony was crucial to George Eliot's development: 'proud, sensitive, bitter, she wandered about Griff, refashioning her world into what she would have liked it to be; the development of her imagination begins with Isaac relinquishing her companionship'.

Such aberrations apart, there is plenty of good sense in Blanche Williams' examination of the influences on George Eliot's young womanhood. She says that, when she freed herself from Maria Lewis, she actually took with her concepts which formed an essential part of her later life: the ideal of duty, the inevitability of effect from cause, the religion of humanity, and her own defined meliorism. Bearing in mind that, when Charles Christian Hennell's *Inquiry Concerning the Origins of Christianity* (1838) was reprinted, George Eliot praised it yet again, Blanche Williams provides a superbly condensed summary of what Hennell actually demonstrated. In view of his great influence on George Eliot, I think it makes essential reading:

> The Gospels are not confirmed by testimony of the Church; they are anonymous; their authorship is far from certain; they were written forty to seventy years after events they profess to record: writers do not tell how they were informed; the four are notably discrepant and contradictory; their tales of miracles cannot be distinguished from the fictions for which every Church finds supporters ready to vouch. Though the account

of the Crucifixion is clear...that of the Resurrection is confused and inconsistent.

Blanche Williams notes that although Hennell is now outdated, his conclusions have not been 'surpassed'. She also refers to Chapman's diary for 1851, saying of Chapman that he made love to 'every woman offering the slightest provocation'. But here she is cautious regarding George Eliot, observing that it is 'Easy to construct in general the affair, dangerous to construct in detail'. She notes the close relationship with Cara Bray and Sara Hennell, quoting Marian Evans' letter of 21 April 1852: 'It is impossible that I should ever love two women better than I love you and Cara.' There is a neat summary of Herbert Spencer's devious activities concerning what Cross should or should not publish about Spencer's role in George Eliot's life, and there is praise for the essay on Heine, because of its finely discriminating distinction between wit and humour.

Concentrating on the fiction, Blanche Williams finds that 'Janet's Repentance' 'is not as good a story as either of its predecessors' and that the Church/evangelical conflict 'is not now very exciting'. Adam Bede receives some detailed appraisal, including the interesting statement that it is 'fused from known scenes. The Hall Farm, for instance, with the gateposts topped by griffins, not lionesses, still stands in Corley Parish, five miles or so from Coventry'. She is also good on notable stylistic differences: 'After the long mellifluous flow of Dinah's speeches, Mrs Poyser's are like whip-cracks.' Blanche Williams' research is not just local, for she finds that a minor work like 'The Lifted Veil' is partly derived from Edgar Allan Poe's 'Facts in the Case of M. Valdemaar': she adds that the story illustrates 'the Comtian doctrine: "I was only suffering from the consequences of a deed which had been the act of my intensest will." ' There is some wise generalisation about some of the novels' major thematic concerns: 'All her books create situations between inclination and duty, situations in which the noble character struggles painfully to the hard right, situations in which the ignoble man or woman yields to the easy wrong.' We might qualify this in degree: in general emphasis it is unquestionably right.

The Mill of course exemplifies this pattern. Silas Marner – 'third of the trilogy treasuring the spirit of that rural England the author loved and remembered' – is praised for its spontaneity, the lack of weighty moralising. There is an appropriate summary of the critical divisions over *Romola* – probably best indicated by the extremes of R.H. Hutton and Lord David Cecil – but Blanche Williams focuses on 'one of the greatest examples of character degeneration in English fiction – natural, inevitable', as she calls Tito. She makes some astute comments on *Felix Holt* which 'is of all her work the plottiest – if the word may be forgiven'. It may, since it appositely defines the needless queries about legal matters which took up so much of her friend, the lawyer Frederic Harrison's time. And from time to time there is an ironic, humorous tone in her consideration: she writes of *The Spanish Gypsy* that it contains 'evidence' that 'she was thinking of woman as mother, thinking in terms that would give disciples of Freud material for essays on her thwarted nature'. Not only Freudian literary analysts, alas, but those of George Eliot's biographers who appear to know her better than they know themselves.

Blanche Williams' criticism of *Middlemarch* – 'Middle Mercia, Coventry' – is characterised by the imagery of the novel itself: 'The novel weaves the stories of three couples; filaments from the rounds of their separate lives meet other rounds, forming a naturally patterned web.' Again there is an intelligent summary of critical differences. With *Daniel Deronda* she evaluates (pre-Leavis) Henry James' 'Conversation', and, although she says of Daniel that George Eliot 'made a dreadful prig', she thinks the novel 'is of all her works the most grandly conceived'. Her final sections are constructed around the word 'passion', used to qualify aspects of George Eliot's life and art. She traces her sufferings in life, in childhood with Isaac, to the death of Lewes in 1878. George Eliot needed passionately to be loved: 'her passion was the condition of her art. To evolve and eternalise a world of beauty was her high purpose'. She was committed to recording the lives of and helping common humanity. Blanche Williams evokes Feuerbach, saying that George Eliot wrote in effect, 'that is a religious marriage which is a true marriage, which corresponds to the essence of marriage – love'. Finally, in *Daniel Deronda*, 'her passion at last broadened to wide sympathy for a race not then popular in England'. She notes her careful use of 'quarries' of material left as mute testimony to 'her preliminary spade-work'. Though she lacks a clear overall perspective, Blanche Williams' commitment to her subject, her awareness of materials, and her

sympathetic but not too subjective identification, prepare the way
for the fuller, more integrated appraisals to come.

Chapter 5
Establishing Values: 1940s-1950s

The first fruits of Gordon Haight's lifetime of research on George Eliot appeared in *George Eliot and John Chapman* (1940), effectively a trailer for *The Letters* (1954-78) and for his 1968 biography. He quotes a sentence from Charles Bray's *Phases of Opinion and Experience During a Long Life* (1885), which has become the most commonly-held view of George Eliot by generations of biographers and critics: 'She was not fitted to stand alone.' While Cross omitted John Chapman from his book, Haight gives details of his life both before, during and after his association with George Eliot. There was her earlier devotion to Dr Brabant: with her arrival in the Strand came her susceptibility to the Byronic Chapman, who shared his affections between his wife and his mistress, the nominal governess Elizabeth Tilley. This is, however, early Haight, and the scholar who has ferreted out the details sits uneasily beside the interpretative mini-biographer anxious to make a point. This, we are told, is what George Eliot felt:

> She loved him more than he knew. What did he find in Elizabeth that she was not prepared to give? Why could he not realise that Elizabeth, in spite of her pretty face, was not worthy of him? The blind rage that George Eliot could never conceal at man's folly in preferring beauty to more substantial qualities surged up in her heart.

Any of George Eliot's millinery biographers, such as Ina Taylor (1989), could (and have) written in this tone. But it is unworthy of Haight, and he rarely offends again.

His account of Chapman's purchase of the *Westminster Review*, of its contributors, of George Eliot's own contributions and of the circles in which she mixed, are all admirable. Haight's overview of the years 1851-3, taking account of the personal, financial and cultural influences which surrounded George Eliot, is a prelude to his more detailed and expansive biography. He also records what seems to me to be of major importance in George

Eliot's development notably Hennell's *Inquiry*, which was 'the precipitating factor that brought her to the conclusion she was never to discard: that Christianity was not a divine revelation, but only the purest form yet existing of natural religion'. Quotations from Chapman's diary (many pages of which were removed) indicate the intensity of her feelings: 'Monday 24 March 1851. M departed today, I accompanied her to the railway. She was very sad, and hence made me feel so. – She pressed me for some inclination of the state of my feelings, – I told her that I felt great affection for her, but that I loved E and S also, though each in a different way. At this avowal she burst into tears.' Two months later Chapman was insensitive enough to raise the subject of 'the incomprehensible mystery and witchery of beauty'. This caused Marian to weep 'bitterly'. 'Was it from a consciousness of her own want of beauty?' There are teasing gaps, and we must take into account Chapman's own capacity for self-dramatisation.

Gerald Bullett (1947) acknowledges the spadework done by Haight and Kitchel, and offers a balanced biographical and critical treatment. There is an interesting evaluation of the Geneva period as marking 'a pause between one life and the next', while Bullett's assessment of Herbert Spencer and his relationship with George Eliot is that he 'seemed not to understand the difference between living reasonably and living by reason'. He also provides an interesting summary of Paul Bourl'honne (1933): Bourl'honne maintained that George Eliot was decisively influenced by the doctrines of Feuerbach in 'marrying' Lewes, and that she bitterly repented this up to her death. As a result she suffered a profound sense of guilt, and her work was a conscious or sub-conscious attempt to expiate this. This is a plausible theory, no more; and Bullett calls Bourl'honne's study a 'psychobiography'. As an interpretation of George Eliot's 'inner life' it can be placed somewhere between Gardner (1912) and Redinger (1975).

Some of Bullett's critical pronouncements are interesting: he rates 'Janet's Repentance' highly, seeing in it 'the clearest promise of what George Eliot was to become'. Bullett has no coherent critical approach; but what he does have is a capacity for provocative assertions: '*Adam Bede* survives even Adam Bede,' or 'If you are a character in a George Eliot novel the chief thing you have to fear is your author's unqualified approval'. Bullett states definitively that *Middlemarch* is 'George Eliot's greatest work', and finds 'an unconscious mastery in her handling of minor episodes' in *Daniel Deronda*.

The impetus arising from the studies of F.R. Leavis (1948) and Joan Bennett (1948) led to increased biographical and critical interest. *Marian Evans and George Eliot* (1952) by Laurence and Elizabeth Hanson is a heavy-weight and somewhat subjective biography with few penetrating cross-references. They acknowledge Haight and draw on the 'new' material available. Their aim is 'to discover and set down the whole George Eliot, not simply one aspect of her'. The treatment is detailed, almost to saturation and certainly predictable, particularly on the early life, where it is safe to call George Eliot a prig, accuse her of misapplying her gifts by compiling a chart of ecclesiastical history, and assert that, although she left 'no mass of evidence' of 'struggles to write', she 'heard, observed, forgot little, said less'. The combined influence of Hennell and Bray is noted; then Brabant, Strauss ('She wept for the loss of Jesus') and through to the death of Robert Evans in 1849. The tone is leisured and well-documented. The Hansons draw parallels between Herbert Spencer's life and Marian Evans' provincial background, evaluate her London experiences on the *Westminster Review*, and say of Lewes that he was 'coarse, and she was not entirely free from coarseness herself'. Their contention is that her translation of Feuerbach helped her to the decision over Lewes: Feuerbach wrote that 'Love is God himself...not a visionary, imaginary Love – no! a real love, a love which has flesh and blood'.

They then turn to the fiction. For the Hansons, *Scenes* is 'an unmistakable poem of the English Midlands with its solid earthy people – yet people discovered to have hearts and minds – little tragedies and high but simple pleasures'. *Adam Bede* is 'the first realistic pastoral novel', drawn from her 'powerful memory' and infused with 'the breadth of her imaginative sympathy'. At the same time, they follow the conventional trend in denigrating the presentation of Adam and Dinah. Mrs Poyser is 'shrew, philosopher, clown, the very salt of the Midland earth'. The remark is almost repeated in the appraisal of the Dodson aunts, 'the very heart of Midland England – a source until then undreamed of in the novel'. Maggie, however, is 'an idealised character', and *Silas Marner* is noteworthy only for its charm. *Romola* shows George Eliot abandoning all that she knows well – 'her knowledge and love

of the Midland places and people'. There is the now usual praise
for the opening of *Felix Holt*, but 'Soon, too soon, Mrs Transome
and all who move about her are relegated to second place'. There
is little else of note and certainly no coherent developed critical
arguments.

The same applies to Robert Speaight (1954), in scope and
approach an introduction to George Eliot along similar lines to
Rosemary Ashton's later, excellent study (1983), though there are
few other points of comparison. Speaight starts at the beginning,
with Griff, 'the warm little nest where her affections were pledged',
and leaps to 'Looking Backward' in *Theophrastus Such* and 'the
influences of the Midland scenery'. Speaight puts George Eliot's
fictional stance in the early novels well: 'It was something deeper
than mere reminiscence; it was a habit of morality and an aptitude
for faith which remained unshaken even when dogmatic belief had
been abandoned and conventional morality had been defied.' He
stresses the fact that it is her 'psychological realism' which is her
'greatest gift'. There is wisdom too in such observations as 'You
feel the grave moral sensibility, the grasp on the primal truths: but
you never feel the obsession of a point of view'. The focus on the
early works generates some beautifully succinct comment, 'These
people create, and are created by, their background; the rich
Midland pastures'. Speaight criticises the unevenness of *Adam
Bede*, implying that here George Eliot is indulging herself, but he
notes her 'growing preoccupation with the nature of tragedy, and
her study of this in the Greek dramatists'. The presentation of the
Mrs Transome-Jermyn relationship is singled out for special
mention, and Speaight draws attention to Leavis' astute
discrimination of this powerful aspect of *Felix Holt*. He sees
Ladislaw as the central flaw in *Middlemarch*; repeats George
Eliot's own assertion, later disproved by Beaty (1960), that 'she
wrote the whole scene' between Rosamond and Dorothea 'without
correction or erasure'. Speaight also notes Leavis' essay on *Daniel
Deronda* (1960) describing his commentary as of 'priceless value'.
He concludes at least with an acceptable generalisation 'What is
remarkable about her [George Eliot] is her sane and total
acceptance of life'.

I have considered Speaight (1954) before Leavis (1948),
undoubtedly the major influence on George Eliot criticism in the
second half of the 20th century, since Speaight pays some

attention to her life. Leavis is concerned with her work and the influences which shaped it. In *The Great Tradition* he places George Eliot squarely with Jane Austen, Joseph Conrad and Henry James in the tradition which cuts across 'complacent confusions of judgment'. These novelists 'are all distinguished by a vital capacity for experience, a kind of reverent openness for life, and a marked moral intensity'; and Leavis traces George Eliot's marked moral influence on Henry James together with her important role in the development of his work. Leavis asserts that George Eliot's own work has to be seen as a whole, indicating how she was influenced by Herbert Spencer and by the disciplined training-ground of her involvement with the *Westminster Review*. She is 'peculiarly addicted to moral preoccupations'. He discusses James' definition of her work as 'a moralised fable', while allowing that *Silas Marner* 'has something of the fairy-tale about it, and is in any case a minor work'. He puts his finger firmly on the pulse of a recognisable shift in critical response: 'what strikes us in the intellectual writer is an emotional quality'. And he summarises admirably certain preconceptions about her, for example that she is generally seen as the novelist of memory, that in her later novels it is commonly held that the intellectual gets the upper hand, while a work like *Romola* is 'the product of an exhausting and misguided labour of excogitation and historical reconstruction'.

Leavis starts with *Scenes*, establishing that, although they hint at the coming great novelist, they have more clumsiness than charm. Yet the compensations are great: for instance, there is 'a lively notation of character, the humour and wit of an acute imaginative observation, and a racy strength of dialogue'. Of *Adam Bede* he notes the idealisation of Adam and Dinah, but feels that the story of Hetty and Arthur is worked in 'with convincing skill'. *The Mill* does not soften or idealise childhood: more important, 'the creative powers at work here owe their success as much to a very fine intelligence as to powers of feeling and remembering'. Yet there is praise too for the 'emotional tone' of the novel and for 'the immediate presence of the author'. This is, however, qualified on a number of counts: the expressive emotional need or hunger 'that shows itself to be insidious company for her intelligence'; the 'self-idealisation' that is present in the character of Maggie; and in such assertions as 'George Eliot shares to the full the sense of Stephen's irresistibleness' (though it is difficult to agree with his judgment here).

Leavis is always interesting, frequently provocative, and sometimes undermined by his own unwieldy constructions: 'The satisfaction got by George Eliot from imaginative participation in exalted enthusiasms and self-devotions would, if she could suddenly have gained the power of analysis that in these regions she lacked, have surprised her by the association of elements it represented.'

Silas Marner's success, we are told, 'is conditioned by the absence of personal immediacy'. True. But when we read that 'charm remains the significant word' in describing it, we wonder if Leavis has read it with the care his wife, Q.D. Leavis, was later to bring to her own edition of the novel (1967). When he gets to the later novels (he dismisses Romola as the 'work of a very gifted mind, but of a mind misusing itself') there is a greater certainty, indeed originality, of critical judgment. Admittedly, there is the needless plot complexity of Felix Holt, and Leavis finds Felix himself a disaster, his mother done out of Dickens, and Rufus Lyon 'incredible and a bore'. But the brilliance and insight of the dialogue between Jermyn and Mrs Transome remain, while 'the theme is profoundly felt and sharply realised'. And here George Eliot becomes 'one of the great creative artists'; the situation 'is presented with complete objectivity'. Leavis has, we feel, penetrated to the layers of psychological truth which characterise George Eliot's insight: as he puts it, by turning limited judgment aside, 'to speak of George Eliot here as a moralist would, one feels, be to misplace a stress'. And he adds 'She is simply a great artist – a great novelist, with a great novelist's psychological insight and fineness of human valuation'. He underlines this by examining Mrs Transome's exchanges with her maid Denner, finding in them 'an astringently moving power unsurpassd in literature'. With Mrs Transome she comes to her full maturity as a 'psychological novelist', while she sees in human mediocrity 'matters for compassion, and her dealings with them are assertions of human dignity'. Leavis concludes that 'To be able to assert human dignity in this way is greatness'.

In his treatment of Middlemarch Leavis is again concerned with personality. He notes the critical 'quality of her irony' (particularly successful in her treatment of Casaubon) and her ability to convey Lydgate's 'intellectual passion as something concrete'. With trenchant independence he says that the weakness of the book lies in Dorothea, and that Ladislaw only exists to 'impose on the reader [George Eliot's] own vision and valuation of Dorothea'. The latter is George Eliot's 'day-dream ideal self'. But it is with *Daniel Deronda* that Leavis comes into his own, and he calls the 'good half' of it 'among the great things in fiction'. At the same time he recognises the self-indulgent nature of the idealism: character is again the centre, with Gwendolen representing the good part of the novel. The influence on James' *Portrait of a Lady* is traced with certainty: 'Isobel Archer is Gwendolen and Osmond is Grandcourt.'

Leavis is particularly revealing on the minor characters, observing 'the fulness of vision and response' present in the conception of Mr Gascoigne. He registers George Eliot's impressive 'grasp of the real', seen in her wide awareness, for example, of the political world, or the society world at the back of her characters: 'What later novelist has rendered the inner movement of impulse, the play of motive that issues in speech and act and underlies formed thought and conscious will, with more penetrating subtlety than she?' It is a large claim, but Leavis demonstrates it with some fine examples of 'psychological notation', most tellingly from Gwendolen's consciousness and in the superb proposal scene with Grandcourt. No later critic, I think, has better expressed the completeness of Gwendolen's fictional conception, and her agony: 'So much pride and courage and sensitiveness and intelligence fixed in a destructive deadlock – that is what makes Gwendolen a tragic figure.'

Leavis' treatment of George Eliot runs to just over 100 pages, and much of this is concerned with establishing her influence on James. There are aberrations, not merely stylistic, as when he says of *Daniel Deronda* that there is 'an actual great novel to be extricated from it'. In reality, we have to take *Daniel Deronda* as it is, and remember George Eliot's own statement that she meant everything in the novel to be interrelated. Leavis is an important influence; independent, brilliantly insightful, bloody-minded, astringent. His achievement in the case of George Eliot can be put quite simply – he showed, by opening up the text, what possibilities it contained, how rich it was, how capable of concentrated investigation which would provide a positive critical yield. He set in train the deep critical preoccupations with George Eliot which characterised the next 40 years and which show no sign of abating.

Joan Bennett's *George Eliot: Her Mind and Her Art* also appeared in 1948. It tends to be overshadowed by Leavis, whose evaluation of George Eliot had first been published in the journal *Scrutiny* in 1945 and 1946. It contains a useful summary of earlier critical responses including W.J. Dawson's in *The Makers of English Fiction* (1905), in which he says that '*Romola* marks her decadence...in *Middlemarch* this decadence is still more pronounced, and it is complete in the utterly tedious *Daniel Deronda*'. In her preface she indicates that George Eliot faced the particular problem of 'how to preserve valuable moral attitudes which were once closely associated with dogma', and she uses the life-story only in relation to the art that developed from it, identifying two enduring traits in George Eliot's nature: 'the passionate force of her affections and the passionate intellectual energy with which she pursues the inquiries those affections suggest to her'. She describes George Eliot's translation of Strauss as 'laborious task work' and, interestingly, gives some attention to her addiction to Spinoza, quoting him with a telling relevance to George Eliot's own concerns: 'How happy would our own age be, could we see religion freed from every kind of superstition,' and defining his belief with regard to religion as being 'to love God above all, and our neighbour as ourselves'. The intelligent use of the biographical material is persuasive. She refers to the letter of 4 December 1849 in which George Eliot wished in her future life 'to have given to me some woman's duty – some possibility of devoting myself where I may see a daily result of pure calm blessedness in the life of another'.

Joan Bennett considers the fiction initially in general terms, feeling that when George Eliot forsakes her chosen provincial sphere she is 'liable to fail'. But 'Within that sphere her sense of humour, her compassion and her moral judgment were unerring'. In fact the sure sense of location is Joan Bennett's main concern. She maintains that the rural and provincial life which George Eliot knew is central – 'her imagination contained it rather than strove after it'. Joan Bennett's main theory is one of outer and inner circles as the distinctive pattern in George Eliot's work – 'The outer circle within which the dramatic situation is contained, is an organic human society, and her novels are deeply imbued with the spirit of a particular place and time'. When George Eliot came to

Middlemarch, therefore, 'with a more assured command of her art, to the environment she mostly understood, she achieved her masterpiece'. Joan Bennett herself analyses particulars, looking closely at Mrs Poyser ('The metaphors that enrich her language spring from the soil in which she was nurtured') and Mrs Holt, and notes 'the humour arising out of intimacy with a tradition'. She indicates how we come to accept the convention of the omniscient author. Her analysis of *Adam Bede* is strongly independent: she considers that there are too many didactic interruptions or asides, that Dinah's semi-biblical idiom is done with 'a distasteful over-carefulness'; but she also believes that Adam is meant to be a prig, and thinks that there is a distance between Hetty, Arthur and the author which reproduces itself somehow between them and the reader.

  The Mill comes in for criticism of its 'grave defects'. She finds the ending poor because 'when we reflect we cannot but feel that this poetic justice at the culminating point of a long, serious, naturalistic novel, is a dishonest contrivance'. In echoing earlier critics here Joan Bennett fails to take account of the meticulous preparations for the ending, the artistic and realistic context of the whole. But she acknowledges that the strength of the novel lies in its being 'the outcome of a child's memories focused and selected by mature intelligence'. There is an apposite quotation from George Eliot's letter to John Blackwood of 28 November 1860 ('the loss of the country has seemed very bitter to me'), but there are some odd critical emphases on *Silas Marner*, where the squirearchy of Raveloe are said 'to belong to a realm of thought and feeling that surrounded her as a child and from which her most untrammelled creative power springs'. In *Romola* she discerns 'a preponderance of discourse about the act over dramatic presentation of the act itself': most critics, of all periods, would I think agree with this. *Felix Holt* is praised in the name of Mrs Transome, and George Eliot, we are told, 'has also recovered and even increased her "negative capability" '.

  On *Middlemarch* and *Daniel Deronda* Joan Bennett is acutely perceptive. On the first she goes back to R.H. Hutton, who referred to its 'delicacy of detail and completeness of finish'. She records the fusion of the two stories but rightly says that the novel is 'a single organism and gives a remarkable impression of unity'. This, too, is important; 'all the surrounding circumstances and characters in *Middlemarch* arise out of that vision of life to which George Eliot attained, in its main features, before she began to write fiction'. She notices constituent elements of *Middlemarch*, evaluating 'the creatures of farce and melodrama' and picking out too the wonderful passage in which Harriet Bulstrode comes to tragic maturity by learning of her husband's guilt. The theme is simply but effectively spelled out: it is 'the adjustment of the aspiring individual to the inhibiting conditions of the actual social world'. From *Daniel Deronda* she selects the conversational exchange between Gwendolen and Grandcourt, which John Blackwood had admired nearly 75 years earlier, saying 'George Eliot indicates the stream of Gwendolen's consciousness as it flows on beneath the conversation between them'.

Joan Bennett's contribution to George Eliot criticism is considerable. The documentation of the early influences is sound, even impressive, and individual insights, such as her theory of inner and outer circles, are important parts of the accumulation of detail which leads to a fuller, deeper critical exploration. This was to come with the next generation of critics, who didn't need to be alerted to George Eliot's greatness because they had discovered it for themselves by reading and re-reading until the patterning became clear, and the powerful fusion of emotion, intellect and imagination involved in the artistic process became evident.

Chapter 6
The Letters in Context

The greatest single contribution to George Eliot scholarship in the 20th century is Gordon Haight's edition of *The Letters* (9 vols, 1954-78); the last two volumes he calls 'frankly supplementary'). The text provides detailed information about the young and intensely Evangelical Mary Ann (later Marian) Evans, her crisis of faith and her refusal to attend church. The influence of the Brays and Hennells can be traced, as well as her work in translating Strauss' *Life of Jesus*. Her life in Geneva, where she went for a few months after her father's death, and, on her return, her relationship with John Chapman and her editing of the *Westminster Review* are also documented. There follows of course, her developing love for Lewes and her departure for Europe with him; their return, her beginning, with his encouragement, to write fiction; the adoption of the pseudonym; success; her correspondence with John Blackwood; and the triumphs which soon followed. The route of the *Letters* from 1854 onwards is from near ostracism to outward acceptance, and from there to eminence and a kind of prophetic status gained through her writings and her personal influence. Thereafter comes the death of Lewes and, 18 months later, her marriage to Cross. Much of this was new, and what was already known was restored from its cautious and sometimes petty manhandling by Cross (1885). From the letters, the journals and notebooks Haight was to produce what is to date easily the best, if rather conservative biography of George Eliot.

One of the chief values of Haight's edition of the *Letters* is that it goes beyond what George Eliot wrote and what was written to her. Haight's dedication meant complete saturation in the period, and his footnotes are an invaluable commentary on this. His informative introduction looks closely at the George Eliot circle, or rather, her ever-widening circles. The introduction sets the tone; the aim is quite simply to put things right, to let Marian Evans, and later George Eliot, speak for herself without any protective editorial bias. Haight sweeps aside many earlier misjudgments and speculations, and his assertion that her letters reflect her width and depth of interests is accurate: 'Her insatiable curiosity embraced all literature, social and political history, science, religion, Bibilical criticism, and philosophy.' His claim is that two-thirds of the text of the *Letters* appears for the first time. He gives a brief but telling resumé of Cross' methods, acknowledging its 'intelligence' but indicating the cuts which helped to present George Eliot as a severe, humourless sybil. Cross did not, in fact, print any of George Eliot's letters in their entirety, and generally tampered with the content and sequence. It has already been suggested that he removed the significant pages of her Journal from 1849-54.

Haight's restorations succeed in showing us 'some of the salt and spice' and confirming 'her intellectual power and her profound moral view of life'. His commentary on George Eliot and her correspondents is superb, and he rates particularly highly those letters written 'during the 1850s after she had thrown off her provincial awkwardness and before the burden of fame weighed her down', though it may be an overstatement to discern in some 'the future novelist practising'. He quotes Basil Willey (1949), who definitively stated that she 'fully epitomises the century; her development is a paradigm, her intellectual biography a graph, of its most decided trend'. Haight next analyses her reading through its various phases, and examines the main strands of her intellectual development from Hennell, through Strauss, the Brays, Herbert Spencer, Comte and Feuerbach. He takes a decisive view of her intellectual interaction with Lewes, saying, 'In the transformation of Marian Evans into a great novelist Lewes had a major part', and he emphasises the psychological, morale-boosting and confidence-protecting which characterised Lewes' endeavours on her behalf. He is equally sure, though, that it would be 'a mistake to believe that George Eliot's mind was deeply influenced by him. Every main bias had been taken before they met, and they respected each other too much to desire uniformity of opinion'. For Haight, George Eliot was 'deeply religious', and he quotes Lord Acton's perceptive statement that her works stand 'as the emblem of a generation distracted between the intense need of believing and the difficulty of belief'. Haight urges us to remember George Eliot's country upbringing in order to under-stand 'many curious contradictions in her life'. Her years in London were haunted by 'The yearning for blue sky, an orchard full of old trees and rough grass': but her greatest need was 'to be understood and approved of'.

Haight's introduction to her correspondents reveals his own meticulous concern with the full and detailed way her life developed as recorded in her extant letters. There are short, telling accounts of her friends at different periods of her life, and of her relationship with her generous publisher, John Blackwood. Prompted by Lewes, he early discovered her touchiness and her need for reassurance. Haight believes that without his support she might not have continued to write fiction. When she defected to Smith Elder for the publication of *Romola*, Blackwood behaved with admirable restraint, 'though other members of the firm took a dark view of her treachery'. Haight presents the friendship between George Eliot and Barbara Bodichon with particular warmth and clarity, outlining the latter's independent, radical and humanitarian career. The sympathy between the two women was 'extraordinary', and Haight recalls Barbara's letter to Marian, whom she recognised in the pages of *Adam Bede*, in which she asserted her 'joy that the novel all the critics were praising was written by a *woman*'. Marian wrote to Barbara of her decision to marry John Walter Cross but the letter was locked in a drawer and not delivered until months later. It did not affect Barbara's generosity: she understood, and said so in the warmest and most direct way.

The influence of Sara Hennell and the Brays and George Eliot's enduring friendship with them is treated succinctly. Haight stresses the enlightened nature of Charles Bray, despite his intellectual fads: he 'agitated courageously for the humane treatment of the insane, secular education, the organisation of trades' unions and workers' co-operatives, extension of the franchise, and for anything tending towards toleration and freedom of speech'. Charles Hennell's marriage to Rufa Brabant, who abandoned the Strauss translation which Marian subsequently took over, is one of the important stages in her development. Sara, Mrs Bray's sister, gave Marian 'the intellectual sympathy' she always needed, but was upset by Marian's liaison with Lewes and, like the others, had no idea that she was the author of *Adam Bede*. Cara Bray too was upset over Lewes, but gradually came round; Marian left her an annuity of £100.

George Eliot's later friendships with women are well-documented. There was Georgiana Burne-Jones, whom she met in 1870, and Mrs Congreve, wife of the founder of the Positivist movement in London. As Haight observes, George Eliot's 'greatest anxiety when she married Cross was how Mrs Congreve would receive the news'. Her husband said that she was 'much pained but bearing up' but remarked that George Eliot 'was not a positivist...Mrs Lewes never accepted the details of the system, never went beyond the central idea'. The Introduction to volume 8 contains a brief study of Edith Simcox, George Eliot's most passionate female worshipper, and in volume 9 Haight includes extracts from her autobiography. Elma Stuart, though not impassioned, was certainly insistent, sending George Eliot a book-slide, the first of her many craftswoman's gifts to her beloved. She was buried next to George Eliot in Highgate Cemetery in 1903, proud that her idol called her 'by the sweet name of "Daughter"'. Haight also gives a valuable account of the Evans family. He mentions the only surviving letter to Marian's father, describing the change in her religious views (28 February 1842), and the letter to Isaac (26 May 1857), informing him that she now has a husband – a letter which drew a reply from the family solicitor. Haight also laconically observes that 'The letters written to Mr and Mrs Samuel Evans at the height of George Eliot's Evangelical fervour are among the unhappiest examples of her epistolary style. The reader may hurry past with the consoling thought that without them we might not have had *Adam Bede*'. The Lewes family is described, with a considered stress on George Henry Lewes and the extraordinary range of his interests and achievements. Haight recalls George Bernard Shaw's valuation of him as 'the most able and brilliant critic between Hazlitt and our own contemporaries'. After briefly discussing the relationship as it developed between Lewes and Marian, Haight demonstrates how Lewes made the practical and protective moves from *Adam Bede* onwards which helped to ensure Marian's achievement as well as her peace of mind. His insight into Marian's becoming a second mother to Lewes' sons is moving. The Cross family, and Marian's intimacy with Johnnie, are traced through the anguish at her loss of Lewes to the marriage and Cross' breakdown/illness on their honeymoon in Venice.

The review of other correspondents is equally revealing, from early exchanges of pedantic piety with her old teacher Maria Lewis onwards. There is the correspondence with Francois D'Albert Durade who gave her lodgings in Geneva for six months in

1849-50, painted her portrait and later translated five of her works into French; with Frederic Harrison, Comtist and lawyer, who advised her on the legal intricacies of the plots of *Felix Holt* and *Daniel Deronda*, and, most notably, with Herbert Spencer, who introduced her to Lewes. But it is not until the Preface to volume 8 that we see the impassioned nature of her feelings for him in the pre-Lewes period (*Letters* VIII, viii).

Haight's commentary is selective but invaluable. His unerring sense of the period, its intellectual, cultural, spiritual and moral ambience is seen in the footnotes to the letters themsleves. References and correspondents alike are identified in nearly every case, and this wide knowledge provides both background and foreground to the life of Marian Evans/George Eliot. Haight's scholarship rarely topples over into pedantry or irrelevance. To read the *Letters* is to follow the life, even with the obvious periods of omission, from fervid Evangelicism, through loss of faith, to the work of the highly competent journalist, the woman sustained by her love, the emergent and then established novelist, and finally the Victorian seer. The footnotes present almost by pleasurable accident, a cultural picture of the times, its rootedness and development. This supplementary material is never boring or obtrusive, and it is accurate, precise scholarship.

There is no need here to focus on individual letters or references, but it is clear that the appearance of the first 7 volumes of the *Letters* in the mid-1950s gave tremendous impetus to both biographical and critical investigations of George Eliot.

Chapter 7
The New Criticism: Elevation

From the late 1950s onwards the pace of critical commentary, scholarly investigation and biographical filling in has been uninterrupted. There has also been an increased interest in George Eliot's background, her friends and her status in our own time. In this highly selective survey I indicate some of the important studies, which established new directions and which still stimulate discussion.

Barbara Hardy's *The Novels of George Eliot: A Study in Form* (1959) inaugurated this new era in George Eliot criticism. By concentrating on what had been relatively neglected or, I am inclined to say, all too readily endorsed – the idea that George Eliot is not 'a great formal artist' – she in fact stressed George Eliot's 'highly complicated and intricate organisations'. Sweeping aside limited conceptions of form, she asserts that 'The novel can gratify the formal pleasure in balance and opposition and unity, and at the same time present its intellectual and moral analysis of men and societies'. This Barbara Hardy explores on a number of levels: through the variously detailed tragic modes: the relationship of character to form; the integration of plot; the author's use of her own voice ('Intimate, Prophetic and Dramatic'); and through other areas, in all of which she reveals the originality of her approach. These areas – the use of image in complex and associative ways, and the might-have-been or could-be resonances in the narrative, which she calls 'Possibilities' – constitute the core of her investigation of form. It is characterised by intellectual awareness and imaginative insight: its method is to isolate, then relate and integrate, the main constituents of George Eliot's art. It establishes subtle usages repeated and varied, which contribute to our aesthetic and emotional satisfaction.

For those who think that such criticism deals only with the text in isolation, it would be worthwhile to look closely at Barbara Hardy's very deliberate perspective: for example, 'George Eliot's composition is usually as complex and as subtle as the composition of Henry James or Proust or Joyce, but it is very much less conspicuous because of the engrossing realistic interest of her human and social delineation'. There follows a definition of form as 'the co-operation of a large number of forms within the novel'. She believes that George Eliot was always concerned with 'balance and continuity', noting that 'She gave up £3000 rather than divide *Romola* into sixteen parts, instead of fourteen, for its serial publication in the *Cornhill*'. She says that George Eliot's world has a 'quiet normality and it is this quietness, which, above all, diverts our attention from its complicated artifice'. It is logical, therefore, for Barbara Hardy to first investigate the early works with their unheroic tragic characters, imbued as they are with George Eliot's 'intensity', and sometimes with 'Her own direct commentary on their behalf', a deliberate 'thematic identification'. She analyses the use of the chorus, examines George Eliot's treatment of violence, notes her 'bids for pathos' and evaluates the 'realistic death-bed' of Dempster's *delirium tremens*. In Hetty Sorrel she asserts 'the egoism of fantasy-life has seldom been more ruthlessly exposed'; but she indicates the quality of George Eliot's encompassing sympathetic tone, which 'softens irony to pity when Hetty plans to kill herself'. There is revealing concentration on the 'methods of understatement' and what she calls 'the free life of realistic fiction...but organised by the intense and driving emphasis of formative vision'.

When Barbara Hardy turns to the tragic process, she says that in George Eliot this is 'a demonstration of human endurance and development'. Her superb analysis of Adam Bede posits that 'Adam's suffering comes out of his rigidity' noting that this is 'stressed by many voices'. Egoism, even in the name of duty, is 'a flaw which tragedy has to mend'. The disability of being a woman in a man's world is seen in the tragic process of the heroines (Romola excepted), with clear pointers to the sketchy education they receive. Men find their vocations, but the heroine is denied such an outlet either in action or opportunity, though 'This does not mean that George Eliot is writing as a proselytising feminist'. The role of the mentor in George Eliot's fiction is evaluated, with particular emphasis on Philip Wakem, strangely neglected by earlier critics according to Barbara Hardy. The theme of affection 'is given a formal and fairly elaborate statement', while an assertion like 'All George Eliot's characters are shown as egoists' is followed by an investigation which ranges from the stereotype through the tragic egoists, the attendant irony, and the expansive 'pattern of variability'. The major characters either develop towards and into altruistic activity, or inwards 'in a slowly hardening egoism which blinds the imagination and moves logically towards the exclusions of betrayal and murder'. The careful reader of George Eliot could ponder the implications of this statement; for me it embraces with greater or lesser degree of emphasis, the whole range of George Eliot's fiction. It occurs in the chapter 'Character and Form', establishing the nature of form and formal awareness at one stroke: it is immediate evidence of Barbara Hardy's saturation in the novels, and of her aesthetic and emotional identification with the recurring states and statements which constitute at once a George Eliot work and all her work.

Contrast and similarity are exposed and, as she says of *Felix Holt*, 'the parallels are in fact designed to meet' or, 'The main source of the concentration of *Middlemarch*...is the correspondence of one plot with another'. Indication of the depth at which her analysis works is seen in her recognition of 'The Morality Play beneath the full rich novel'. In *Middlemarch* particularly there is the involvement of the minor characters in the structure, with both simplified pointers and deeper layers of connection evinced in its book titles. Dealing with plot, Mrs Hardy examines the force of the 'repeated situation'.

I suggest, however, that it is her chapter VII, 'Possibilities', which explains and develops a most exciting and omnipresent aspect of George Eliot's art, the might-have-beens in her creative imagination which are silently but insistently there. She instances the hinted possibility of Gwendolen's having a son in *Daniel Deronda*, with all the complications this would have generated. There are a number of 'attempted and rejected variants', and an analysis of similarity and difference in fact and decision between Esther and Mrs Transome in *Felix Holt*. The opposite examples of Maggie and Tito in crisis are shown, while Gwendolen's anguished experience of temptation is given a warmly sympathetic exposure. Barbara Hardy considers that the 'possible' coming together of Dorothea and Lydgate, which some reviewers of the early part issue felt was desirable (and which obviously many readers wanted or expected) is 'there as a faint stirring of irony'. There is a close look at temptation as 'drifting', while a wide range of association encompasses such characters in *Middlemarch* as Fred, Mary and Mr Farebrother in their 'imagined otherwise'. Barbara Hardy asserts, then demonstrates, that 'The world of unrealised possibility is most prominent in *Daniel Deronda*'.

She next examines George Eliot's various uses of her own authorial voice, starting with that 'of personal knowledge and recollection', which is 'nostalgic and reminiscent'. There is some striking quotation from the last four novels to illustrate the combination of 'the reflective tone with the bid for sympathy', and there is one assertion – 'The compassion never dies out of George Eliot's commentary' – which seems to me to underline Barbara Hardy's own response to George Eliot's personal humanity. The prophetic voice, from the casual to the subtle, is expressively registered, and the clarity with which this is used in *Romola* shows the novelist's awareness of the part it plays in the structural cohesion of her works. We share the fascination these evidences of George Eliot's formal subtlety exert, whatever the shortcomings of *Romola* may be.

The modes of George Eliot's dramatic immediacy range from Hetty's physical journey, with its corollary in terms of consciousness, through to Gwendolen's 'oscillating between intention and desire'. And the appraisal of Bulstrode moves from the flat presentation to the inward; then 'Bulstrode, like Tito, is withdrawn from our view, and the convention of omniscience suspended. The voice is as expressive in its absence as in its presence'. This is followed by an examination of the various types of scene, particularly those of solitude, which become more 'elaborate' as backgrounds to individual crises: the 'disenchanted day-lit' room is a recurring one. The variety of functions of the imagery is stressed, with both variants and progression in that of wounded animal and bird, flower and seed, and then of the child or youth, with differing degrees of pathos. In the last two novels there is 'a Shakespearian use of running images', while the 'ironical converse' is seen at its fullest in *Middlemarch* – 'the image of the water, the image of the dark or narrow place, and the image of the mirror'. The importance of Barbara Hardy's conclusion for all readers of George Eliot seems to me indisputable:

> George Eliot's formal subtlety is something which places her in a special relation to the writing of our own century...because it finds an expression for themes which are close to the themes

of novelists and poets of our time...she saw within the human condition the possibilities of a humanity which could be its own providence...she tries to measure the individual life against the flow of history, showing society as shaping and being shaped by each of its human units.

The last sentences of the study are a definitive tribute to George Eliot, which also indicate, for this reader at least, the sympathetic affinity with her that Barbara Hardy's own writing displays:

> She shows all the human variables: the successes as well as the failures, the mixed cases, even the unacted possible lives that haunt all our commitments. The result is moral definiteness, maybe, but it is also human movement. We are left with the impression, after reading one of her novels, that this is as close as the novelist can get to human multiplicity – that here form has been given to fluidity and expansiveness. We can trace the form as we can trace a diagram, but the form is always there in the interest of the human picture.

Re-reading A Study in Form some thirty years on, one can't help feeling that its vibrant interpretations of George Eliot's works have not dated, though Barbara Hardy's investigation of further 'particularities' was still to come.

Published in the same year, Jerome Thale's The Novels of George Eliot (1959) bears some resemblance to Barbara Hardy's work, which it acknowledges, along with Joan Bennett and F.R. Leavis. But there is little depth to this fragmented writing: Thale says that 'Brother Jacob' is 'an awkward attempt at farce', while he is deliberately provocative when he asserts that the development of George Eliot's work 'is towards decreasing intellectuality'. What he really means, as he says a little later, is 'not so much that George Eliot became less intellectual but that her art became better'. There is some justice in saying that Mrs Poyser, successful though she is, 'is a little too much tried for', but overall, there is too much descriptive criticism and some wrongheadedness. The essay on The Mill is a defence rather than a critique – 'the distinction between the author and [Maggie] is not always clear to the reader'. Silas Marner embodies two visions, the fable of Silas and the reality of Godfrey Cass. True. But to follow this by commenting that only here did she 'find a way to present the two visions of the world as one artistic piece' seems to me very limiting and limited. Thale says of Middlemarch, 'But why it is great it is not easy to say'. Again true; but the business of criticism is surely to illuminate the aspects of a work which make for greatness. Thale's sequence of essays is not without critical merit. He looks closely at the text and, though some of the conclusions are dubious, they are direct and sometimes stimulating appraisals, while lacking the overview and the incisive particularity of Barbara Hardy's approach.

Reva Stump's *Movement and Vision in George Eliot's Novels* (1959) is more successful, though limited in perspective, as the title perhaps implies. In essence it examines *Adam Bede*, *The Mill* and *Middlemarch*. The 'dramatic action...for the most part derives its tension from the contradictory urges to see and to avoid seeing'. Vision is of course a relative not an absolute term, and is followed through its application to *Adam Bede*, from the first sunlit scene, through Dinah's eyes (and the language of her preaching), to the counter movement of Arthur and Hetty with their lack of both sight and insight, the negative side of vision. Contrasts with Dinah are emphasised, but Hetty's journey is given due symbolic weighting in a fine piece of visual and associated analysis.

The positive movement is seen in the development of Adam, his 'slow and painful progression' towards 'the art of vision'. Especially good is the section dealing with the way he 'shrinks from seeing Hetty', while a partial vision of the consequences of their actions comes to Hetty and Arthur. In *The Mill*, Reva Stump sees George Eliot as being engrossed with 'the nature of moral vision', as she was in *Adam Bede*, and here the negative and positive movements produce 'a constant tension'. The animal imagery here is given detailed treatment, being seen as 'a means of character-ising and defining temperaments'. Full human responses (productive) are set against the destructive responses of a 'rigid society'. She sees the conclusion of *The Mill* as its weakness, but in examining its antithetical movements she gives an excellent analysis of Philip's 'new life', entered through loving Maggie despite having lost her. Tom, in contrast, represents 'the fullest extension of the movement away from vision'. Reva Stump stresses that 'the flood scene is a symbolic enactment of Maggie's life, of the movement from darkness to light, from blindness to vision'. In *Middlemarch* she examines the governing metaphor of the novel, 'this particular web', before proceeding to 'The Window and the Web'. Much of her work interacts independently with

Barbara Hardy's. Dorothea's development is traced: the textual intensity is such that we follow the 'movement' to 'vision' with a corresponding excitement. This is good criticism, taking us back and into the novel. Much is made, rightly, of the scene betweeen Dorothea and Rosamond, *and its effects* (my italics), in ch. 81 of the novel.

W.J. Harvey's *The Art of George Eliot* (1961) concentrates on 'the methods of the art and the nature of the organisation', thus stressing 'the formal characteristics of her work'. He and Barbara Hardy ensured that their work did not overlap: his Introduction states that 'we have reached much the same conclusion but, I think, by different routes'. Harvey believes – and he was certainly right – that there was going to be 'a great leap forward in our understanding and appreciation of Victorian fiction'. At the same time he believes that the 'new' discoveries (he instances symbolic usage in Dickens) should not be allowed to obscure traditionally accepted excellences.

He concentrates initially on George Eliot's ability to extend our moral insight and sympathy 'through the agency of the imagination working upon particulars'. He looks closely at the varying treatments of egoism, which 'constitute a large though negative part of the moral burden of her novels'. Her idealistic philosophical position is also stressed, and he notes that 'her variety of determinism is not crude or mechanical; it is subtle and flexible'. George Eliot recognises and embodies in her work an understanding of complex relations, she knows that 'life is rarely a matter of simple categories'. Harvey is very good on 'the moral enlargement' of George Eliot's characters, as well as 'the sharply defined stances', such as Casaubon 'in the posture of death'. Aspects of omniscience are explored, including that of intrusion, for example George Eliot's use of the 'historic present'. An instance of this is where Arthur gallops up with the reprieve for Hetty. In *Middlemarch* she 'achieves the steadiness and clarity of ironic comtemplation'.

One very interesting emphasis is on George Eliot's own critical concern for her work, seen in her letters to, among others, R.H. Hutton and Bulwer Lytton. He also covers the main flashback technique of 'Mr Gilfil's Love Story' and the typicality of the opening of *Felix Holt*, where she takes care 'to establish a stable temporal relationship between the present and the past world which was generally her subject'. He also indicates her 'complex' 'control of historical perspectives', the establishing of unity through time in *Daniel Deronda*, and examines 'the many modes of anticipation' in the novels. Background characters who have a largely functional role are discussed, and from there he proceeds to the protagonists. This is largely a concentration on limited or unsuccessful portrayals, though Harvey credits George Eliot with trying to 'check the idealisation of Dinah'. There is some telling investigation of 'character-as-relationship' interaction and, for instance, its deficiency in *Romola*. And as with so many other critics, he finds Mordecai 'an almost entirely theoretical character', while Ladislaw 'crumples under the weight of the symbolic value with which he is laden'. Dorothea and Maggie are over-idealised. There is a consideration of imagery and the nature of George Eliot's prose, which he finds 'Johnsonian rather than Jamesian in its affiliations'. Her use of imagery is 'increasingly economic'.

In *Religious Humanism and the Victorian Novel* (1965), U.C. Knoepflmacher notes that George Eliot successfully 'transmuted ideas into the form and structure of her novels'. He maintains that any analysis of, for example, imagery, must first seek out the intellectual derivations. Here he looks back to Feuerbach, and then concentrates on what he regards as the three major aspects of her thought 'which went into the making of her novels: her scientific positivism, her "humaniastion" of Christianity, and her Arnold-like belief in the force of tradition'. He believes that the early novels contain a deceptive pastoralism: the characters are not judged by a static 18th-century standard, 'but in terms of the dynamic world-picture provided by the "Development theory" '. He explains that her 'reluctant acceptance of the "relative" man of biological science had been preceded and, to some extent, prepared for by her earlier assent to the "relative" Christ of the "Higher Criticism"'. He suggests, it seems to me correctly, that the translation of *The Life of Jesus*, far from stilling her religious questioning, only added to it. Later, however, she could say, (*Letters* II, 153) 'With the ideas of Feuerbach I everywhere agree'. He refers to Feuerbach's argument that his 'sole purpose was the revitalising of symbols that Christianity had objectified', and says that George Eliot in her fiction created the truth that Christianity was a beautiful fable. In this context there is some first-rate explication of the 'symbolic suppers' in *Adam Bede*.

George Eliot's own sympathetic creed is well in evidence, one feels, before her translation of Feuerbach's *Essence of Christianity* (published 1854), and after her early fiction she sought 'a compelling vehicle for her ideals'. Knoepflmacher gives a detailed exploration of heart and mind in *Middlemarch*, with particular reference to Lydgate and Dorothea. And he underlines the structure by observing that 'Balance is all in *Middlemarch*. George Eliot the rationalist corrects George Eliot the enthusiast; Dorothea the enthusiast corrects Lydgate the rationalist'. As he puts it, 'no other novel before *The Ambassadors* uses complementary points of view to a greater effect'. Knoepflmacher offers a mature appraisal throughout this important and enlightened investigation. For him *Middlemarch* 'is neither tragedy nor comedy. It is the tragi-comedy of human progress. The essential difference between the last two novels is that *Middlemarch* illuminates the past for the benefit of the present; it is analytical, prosaic and, for the most part, detailed. *Daniel Deronda*, written only five years later, examines the present, but ardently longs for the future'.

Chapter 8
Life and Art: Biography and Scholarship

Jerome Beaty's *Middlemarch: From Notebook to Novel* (1960)
was a pioneering study of George Eliot's *Quarry* and manuscript
for the novel. An important investigation, it focuses on the
preparation for writing, the writing itself, and what we can learn
from these. Beaty points out that 'the first eighteen chapters of
Middlemarch are a fusion of the beginnings of two separate prose
works'. He examines original beginnings and different versions,
and he also indicates the influences and the changes brought
about by part-publication, then links the notebook to 'the resultant
portions of *Middlemarch*'. A detailed examination follows of the
revisions from chapter 81 – the dramatic and emotional scene
when Dorothea visits Rosamond the day after she has seen her
with Will. Because of George Eliot's quoted account of how she
came to write this chaper – cited so often by critics as evidence
that her best work was done at a white heat of emotion – this is
given special consideration.

The earlier *Middlemarch* was begun in July 1869 – it lacked
Dorothea, Casaubon and Ladislaw, but the 'Miss Brooke' part
dates from December 1870. By March 1871 it is clear that 'my
Novel' had obviously incorporated the separate parts. Eighteen
chapters were completed: Beaty here indicates the importance of
the manuscript, even noting the 'differences of the paper stocks'
as indications of the times at which the changes were made. He
suggests that the 'similarity of theme' was in part responsible for
George Eliot joining the Lydgate-Dorothea stories, and then
proceeds to a close analysis of the early chapters. It is a fascinating
piece of composition-detection and, if not conclusive in every
detail, establishes with some certainty the order of writing, revision
and change.

In relation to the Parts, Beaty examines the *Quarry for
Middlemarch* (ed. A.T. Kitchel, 1950), which includes George
Eliot's planning of 'How to End the Parts'. This was subsequently
changed in order to fit in with the way the novel developed. Beaty

indicates the correlations between *Quarry* and manuscript: as he puts it, 'The net effect of Parts publication was, in fact, to aid George Eliot in the fusion of "Miss Brooke" and *Middlemarch*', but he points out that there were many difficulties in achieving complete unity. He then widens the investigation to include the headings used by George Eliot in the *Quarry* (called *Quarry II*, because the notebook was turned over and the second half used). He documents the writing of the novel. Lewes' suggestion that the last two parts should be published monthly instead of bi-monthly is noted and 'The more quickly George Eliot wrote, it seems, the more numerous were her notebook plans'. Book Six has more plans than any other. Beaty comments, however, on the lack of success in the integration of characters like Raffles and Rigg, who are 'incompletely visualised, incompletely presented. The coincidences are too many'. But Book Seven was written quickly, probably because 'the plans for the earlier parts had been extensive enough to cover the development of the last parts of the novel'. In these last sections there is strong evidence for the continuing process of 'change and enrichment' from the plans, though a marked degree of haste is evident in the composition of the final book.

Chapter 81 is 'a truly *Middlemarch* chapter' since it comes well after the fusion of the two stories, and it is also the result of a complex process of revision, clearly not simply derived from inspirational passion. George Eliot magnified the unconscious element in the composition of this chapter: Cross reported that in the scene when Dorothea is in Rosamond's drawing-room, George Eliot 'abandoned herself to the moment, she wrote the whole scene exactly as it stands, without alteration or erasure, in an intense state of excitement and agitation, feeling herself entirely possessed by the feelings of the two women'. *Quarry II* makes it clear that the scene was planned, though there are few details. The manuscript proves that 'this chapter was more heavily revised than most of the others in *Middlemarch*, and Beaty examines minor changes, deliberate tactical alterations, evidence of sensitivity to structure: there is a very thorough realisation of the character of each woman. Both notebook and manuscript contradict Cross' statement. As Beaty puts it, 'She made changes in every stage of writing and of almost every possible extent. She made changes in matters of style and changes in the matter itself'. And he emphasises the care with which she treated Rosamond's 'out of character' confession to Dorothea. George Eliot was neither mechanical nor unpremeditating. Her writing 'was a process of evolution and discovery'.

The importance of Beaty's work cannot be overstressed. With all the notebook manuscripts available, from the publications beginning with *Quarry* in 1950 through to the present time, the scope of Eliot's creative methods, from manuscript drafts through editions in her lifetime, can be examined and her ideas, composition and revisions, charted. Beaty paved the way, and his work is a signal example of dedicated detection, a genuine expansion of our knowledge of George Eliot.

During the 1960s there were similar advances in three other areas; background, the essays and most important of all, Haight's biography. K.A. McKenzie's *Edith Simcox and George Eliot* (1961) is a well-documented account of Edith Simcox' passionate devotion to George Eliot after their meeting in 1872. Her 'Autobiography of a Shirt Maker' unavailable until 1958, is extensively referred to by Haight, and McKenzie inspires interest in Edith for her own sake. She had a discerning, versatile critical intelligence, was intent on improving the lot of women workers, and there is little doubt that Lewes encouraged her worship of George Eliot because it helped to counteract her [George Eliot's] 'self-depreciation and diffidence'.

Haight's introduction to McKenzie's study says that where the Victorians saw 'beautiful friendship, the modern reader suspects perversion'. George Eliot never returned Edith's feelings and told Edith that the friendship of men meant more to her than that of women. But Edith continued to pour out her heart, writing 'My Sweet Darling', 'My own beautiful love' and 'every night what has been done ill or left undone shall be confessed on my knees to my Darling and my God'. Edith Simcox is the extreme example of George Eliot's power to attract adoration or love in women. Jealous of Cross' influence, she was drawn towards Lewes, and projected a biography of George Eliot which was forestalled when Cross made his own plans known. The eroticism and pathos of her utterances are almost unbearably extreme. McKenzie discerns a masculine quality in her love for George Eliot. As late as 1887 (seven years after George Eliot's death) she recalled once restraining herself when she saw Lewes and George Eliot together:

she wanted to 'kiss first one and then the other as a parent does two happy children'. George Eliot may have enjoyed the worship, but Edith Simcox herself gives evidence that she rejected its expression: once after a passionate kissing of the feet, Edith found the footstool withdrawn for the rest of the evening! Edith Simcox also suggested that George Eliot was so uncertain about marrying Cross that she twice broke it off as impossible. Her influence on Edith was such that it supplied 'the principal drive for her labours towards social amelioration', and Edith Simcox' valedictory article in the *Nineteenth Century* is her fullest public tribute to her goddess: 'precious as the writings of George Eliot are and must be always, her life and character were yet more beautiful than they'.

Haight's biography appeared in 1968, when he had been working on George Eliot for some 35 years. After detailing the major sources for his work, his emphasis is on the influence exerted by her background and her yearning, throughout her time in London, for 'blue sky, orchards full of old trees and tough grass...' He describes her earliest extant fiction, 'Edward Neville', and shows the importance of her father's death in 1849 to her subsequent development. When she went to Geneva, shortly afterwards, she began a Journal, which she kept for the next 11 years, though only the entries for the period after she began living with Lewes survive.

We are still on familiar ground, but Haight's scrupulous documentation ensures that, as we trace Marian's life, we also feel the effect of its various phases set in the provincial or early London/ Geneva contexts. His commentary on her editing of ten issues of the *Westminster Review* is of great interest, and he notes that it was her responsibility to link the various contributions together, and that therefore her touch can be found in reviews she did not actually write. He advocates caution in making definitive attributions of articles to her. Haight surveys every detail of her life, even recording, for example, Bessie Rayner Parkes' testimony to the accuracy of Mayall's 1858 portrait photograph. He treats with irony Spencer's exaggerated concern for his own health and his sensitivity on the subject of Marian when Cross was compiling the *Life*: Marian's feelings for Spencer were those of 'an ardent, generous nature offering herself to an egoist who could love nothing but his "image" '. Haight is also cautious over the question of free-love so often associated with Lewes, observing 'So far as I can discover, the Hunts and the Leweses, though they undoubtedly spent much time together, never lived under the same roof'. He identifies clues of the early intimacy of Lewes and George Eliot: Lewes reviewed Thornton Hunt's *Religion of the Heart* in the *Leader* and added 'a curious sentence'; 'All we can say is, that a noble and accomplished woman was listening to her husband's reading of the book when we called one evening, and her eyes were full of tears'. Haight's comment demonstrates the unevenness of his own appraisal. He observes 'The adjectives fit Marian well; he would hardly apply them to Agnes, Lewes' wife, just delivered of her third bastard. Was the caller beginning to think of himself as Marian's husband?' Or was he just fantasising with his usual histrionic verve? Haight is generally tentative, but he occasionally indulges a whim, as here.

He is particularly good, though, in tracing the correlation between Feuerbach's thought and George Eliot's own intellectual development: 'Love is God himself, and apart from it there is no God...marriage as the free bond of love – is sacred in itself, by the very nature of the union which is therein effected.' He draws heavily on the *Letters* to show George Eliot's feelings for the Brays and Sara (and her sister Chrissey). He suggests that the 'easy allusiveness' of her novels can be traced to her close reading, but asserts that 'Truth was her aim, psychological truth, as well as truth of background to make her story plausible'. Haight always provides detail on her reading habits.

After her letter to Isaac in 1857, Marian was upset when her sister Chrissey and her half-sister Fanny broke off communication with her. Haight (p. 238) turns to *Scenes*, indicating how certain aspects of 'Janet's Repentance' were softened, and records the reviews of *Scenes* and *Adam Bede*. He also comments on 'the remarkable density of background her realism achieves' in *Adam Bede*. His own praise of the novel is unequivocal – 'No book had made such an impression since *Uncle Tom's Cabin* swept the world'. At this stage Haight's own narrative picks up the excitement, recording the astonishment of Cara and Sara when Marian told them she was the author of *Adam Bede*. She had not yet revealed this publicly, and the gossip column of the *Athenaeum* contained the accusation that the question of the identity of the author was an 'elaborate attempt to mystify the reading public. No woman of genius ever condescended to such a *ruse*, – no book was ever permanently helped by such a trick'.

Occasionally, Haight ventures critical commentary, seeing in 'The Lifted Veil' an early precursor of Virginia Woolf's stream of consciousness technique, which gives it 'a curiously modern quality'. Generally, though, he keeps to his chosen area. He selects a letter from Mrs Congreve (1 May 1859) to show how even at this early stage George Eliot exerted a strong attraction on other women. He takes a direct attitude towards the supposed influence of Comte: 'The extent of George Eliot's concern with Positivism has been greatly exaggerated.' There are some touching indications of the intimacy between George Eliot and Lewes, who inscribed a copy of Chappell's *Popular Music of the Olden Time* 'To Her who makes the music of my life. From G.H. Lewes Feby 1860'. And there is, of course, Lewes' influence on *Romola*: he suggested 'an historical romance' based on Savonarola's life and times, and 'Polly at once caught at the idea with enthusiasm'. Without connecting critically with the novels, Haight always registers imaginatively their local impact, wondering, for example, how the Warwickshire relatives would react to 'We hear a voice with the very cadence of our own uttering the thoughts we despise' from ch. 4 of *Adam Bede*. He also notes what Mathilde Blind saw in Lawrence's portrait of George Eliot, both the 'powerful sensual element' and 'the cold, subtle, and unconscious cruelty of expression which might occasionally be detected there'.

Haight's strength, as I have indicated, lies in his meticulous attention to detail. Just as George Eliot accumulated masses of material in her researches for *Romola*, so Haight accumulates the vast reading programme she undertook. And he has his own irony, speculating as to what Lewes, (who claimed that you only need to know Scott, then cram period stuff in order to write a historical novel) felt about George Eliot's 'grubbing through collections of Tuscan proverbs to cull archaic colloquial phrases...' Haight chooses telling quotations about *Romola* from its author, who spoke of 'every sentence as having been written with my best blood, such as it is, and with the most ardent care for veracity of which my nature is capable', and who also said 'My own books scourge me'. Blackwood's correspondence indicates that he believed Lewes' greed to be responsible for her defection to Smith Elder for the publication of *Romola*. But heavily dependent on Lewes she certainly was. Her journal entry for 25 March 1865 says of him, 'How I worship his good humour, his good sense, his affectionate care for every one who has claims on him! That worship is my best life'.

There is interesting and full documentation on the conception of *Felix Holt*, with its childhood recall of the Nuneaton election riots and her classical reading which, as Fred Thomson (1959) pointed out, shows that Mrs Transome rather than the political plot was central to the conception. Frederic Harrison's exaggerated praise of *Felix Holt* (he knew 'whole families where the three volumes have been read chapter by chapter and line by line and reread and recited as are the stanzas of *In Memoriam*') draws a rare sliver of humour from Haight, who calls this 'a hyperbole that attests his admiration, though it makes one marvel at his friends!' Haight notes how Lewes promoted George Eliot, fostering her need for acceptance and recognition, 'bringing the great of the world to her door'. He stresses her increasing conservatism (she would not contribute to the Mazzini fund), and commenting on 'Felix Holt's Address...' he calls him 'that most conservative radical'.

Haight describes how the Priory, Regents Park, which George Eliot and Lewes had moved to in 1863 became the centre of the most interesting society in London: he also gives James' account: 'To begin with she is magnificently ugly – deliciously hideous...in this vast ugliness resides a most powerful beauty...so that you may end, as I ended, in falling in love with her.' As she moved towards the stories that were to be fused in *Middlemarch*, she was beset by the death of Lewes' son Thornie ('This death seems to me the beginning of our own') and by thinking back to her childhood in Warwickshire. The 'Brother and Sister' sonnets were the result. Haight covers Lewes' innovatory plans for bi-monthly publication of *Middlemarch* and notes the laudatory reviews, particularly Edith Simcox'. He comments that, like her great contemporaries, George Eliot exposed the nature of a society that was dominated by wealth, and briefly, he indicates inconsistency, saying of *Daniel Deronda* that her 'frank avowal of didacticism' contradicts her 'basic tenet that fiction should represent real life'. The increasing attachment of women to George Eliot is instanced by the love-letter of an American admirer: 'You will not be bored by another love-letter – a little one?...Don't answer this, dearest...I *love* you, you are so love-worthy,' and he quotes Geoffrey Tillotson's note of caution on Edith Simcox, which suggested that she mingled fact and fantasy.

The final phase includes *Daniel Deronda* and Lewes' death in 1878. Afterwards George Eliot copied all 8 stanzas of Emily Brontë's 'Cold in the Earth' into her Diary. Haight records how touched and delighted she was by being called 'Sister' by the Cross clan. There is her moving response to her brother's letter of congratulation – 'our long silence has never broken the affection for you which began when we were little ones'. Haight reiterates her conservatism, her need for the final conformity of her marriage to Cross. And of the latter he notes his 'sudden mental derangement' in Venice, which has been made so much of by lesser biographers. Haight (1968) is perhaps the definitive biography of George Eliot to date. Its documentation, insight and broad tolerance more than compensate for unevenness and reticence. Here there is of course no Cross-style cover-up, but rather a sense of responsibility and integrity, which makes him report facts and discuss speculation, but avoid the sensational and meretricious.

Thomas Pinney's edition of the *Essays of George Eliot* (1963) is invaluable on a number of counts. He points out that before her death she revised certain essays which appeared in *Essays and Leaves from a Notebook* (1884), and he maintains that this gives an imperfect idea of the nature and variety of her writings, that her revisions detracted from their liveliness. He therefore prints the essays here in their original versions. His introductions and comments are excellent, and his exemplary sense of period, background and modest pointers to a review/essay/article's significance give his methods the stamp of authenticity. He describes George Eliot's style as allusive, often with 'humour and real wit in her comments on books and men'. During her editorship of the *Westminster Review* (1851-4) she herself contributed reviews, though no essays, but she later wrote the 'spacious reviews' typical of the period. Her later essays for the *Westminster* show her tackling questions on which she believed she had something of importance to say; in those on Cumming and Young for example, she set out to demolish her subjects. The sympathetic essays are on Heine and Riehl, where her beliefs and her later fictional practice come through: 'art teaches not by preaching but by a sympathetic and imaginative presentation'. Pinney indicates her range of review, including the articles for the *Leader*. Briefly, he concludes that the articles 'contain much that is directly relevant to the study of the novelist'.

Some of George Eliot's reviews yield important statements. Thus in Mackay's *The Progress of the Intellect* (*Westminster*, liv, 1851) she praises him and refers to 'the inexorable law of consequences...human duty is comprised in the earnest study of this law and patient obedience to its teaching'. In Carlyle's *Life of Sterling* she indicates what she considers a biography should be – a real life 'setting forth briefly and vividly the man's inward and outward struggles, aims, and achievements, so as to make clear the meaning which his experience has for his fellows'. We can't help feeling the irony here in the retrospective light of Cross' practice in her own case. An indication of her range is seen in 'Liszt, Wagner and Weimar', where, as Pinney observes, there is one of the 'earliest friendly comments on Wagner in the English press'. Her description of Liszt anticipates her portrayal of Klesmer in *Daniel Deronda*: 'with head thrown back and nostril dilated...But, take him all in all, he is a glorious creature'. She reviews Geraldine Jewsbury's *Constance Herbert*, taking her to task for saying that what duty calls upon us to 'renounce will inevitably prove "not worth the keeping"; and if it *were* the fact, renunciation would cease to be moral heroism, and would be simply a calculation of prudence'. The heavyweight essays are complemented by a delightful lightness of touch in some of the reviews: having castigated Brougham's hack biographies, she says that his 'lives had already been depicted in all sorts of ways, and presented to us in all sorts of lights – like Prince Albert's legs'. In 'The Morality of *Wilhelm Meister*' she praises Goethe's 'mode of treatment', which is 'really moral in its influence'.

The attack on Cumming, according to Charles Lee Lewes' report of his father's judgment, showed her 'true genius'. There is a fine rhetorical flow about the writing, and two points of the attack, those on *the absence of genuine charity* and on *perverted moral judgment* anticipate aspects of her own thematic stance as a writer of fiction. In this article we also find the assertion that 'the tendency towards good in human nature has a force which no creed can utterly counteract'. Reviewing Tennyson's *Maud* she writes (of *In Memoriam*) that 'the deepest significance of the poem is the sanctification of human love as a religion'. Of Margaret Fuller she says 'But we want freedom and culture for woman, because subjection and ignorance have debased her'.

If these extracts indicate her range, then the article 'German

Wit: Heinrich Heine' shows her sensitivity and sympatheic insight as well as her critical maturity. Pinney points out that George Eliot is 'one of the leading sponsors of German thought and art in 19th-century England'. In his poetry Heine is 'no echo, but a real voice'; he has 'poetic imagination', 'wit, humour, and just thought'; he 'indicates a whole sad history in a single quatrain'. Of 'The Natural History of German Life', Pinney advocates reading it in conjunction with Felix Holt's 'Address to Working Men'. It symbolises the Wordsworthian belief that the 'highest function of art is the extention of our sympathies' towards 'the life of the people'. It is in this essay that George Eliot condemns the cockney sentimentality of certain paintings: she also attacks the distant idyll perspective of rustic life, substituting the realism of fact for the effluence of fancy: 'the only realm of fancy and imagination for the English clown exists at the bottom of the third quart pot'. This is followed by a definition of her creed: 'Art is the nearest thing to life; it is a mode of amplifying experience and extending our contact with our fellow-men beyond the bounds of our personal lot.' She then emphasises our need to feel for 'the peasant in all his coarse apathy, and the artisan in all his suspicious selfishness'. Of 'Silly Novels by Lady Novelists' Pinney observes that, right at the beginning of her own career as a novelist, she affirms the limitations often present in women novelists. Her definitions of the 'mind and millinery species', of the 'oracular species' and of the 'white neckcloth species' sufficiently indicate her satirical tone: she is moved to say 'The real drama of Evangelicalism – and it has abundance of fine drama for anyone who has genius enough to discern and reproduce it – lies among the middle and lower classes'. She herself was about to show the genius and reproduce the drama. When she came to condemn the 'modern-antique species' she wrote 'the finest effort to reanimate the past is of course only approximative – is always more or less an infusion of the modern spirit into the ancient form'. But this, of course, was some five years before Lewes suggested *Romola* to her. Of the Swedish writer Frederika Bremer she praised her 'most solid sort of Dutch realism', while deploring her 'vapourishly affected and unreal' situations and bigoted theories. Of the fine essay on Young, Pinney says that 'the principle of truth to feeling, an idea of eternal importance in the ethics and art of George Eliot, is the basis of her argument'.

Chapter 9
Feminist and Other Studies

Marghanita Laski's *George Eliot* (1973) is easily the best illustrated biography of the novelist we have. The emphasis on the early life is clear-cut: 'by the time that Mary Anne left Griff House, she had amassed all the material for George Eliot's earlier novels, and much that was to serve her up to the last one'. But as this study unwinds we become aware that Marghanita Laski is not ena-moured of her subject, or at least, her subject's personality. She uses the letters with great care however, referring to Mary Anne's brief (supposed) romance with the young picture-restorer and to the superb fantasy letter of October 1846 (*Letters* VIII, 12-13) about 'a dry as dust German professor who came to England in search of a wife; she must be ugly, a competent translator, and possessed of a little capital, and the professor found his ideal in Coventry in Mary Ann Evans'. It is a refreshing note from that self-absorbed period of her life.

Marghanita Laski is even less taken with Lewes. She refers often to Eliza Lynn Linton, well-known for her hostility towards Lewes and George Eliot, and reports her unsubstantiated story of Mary Anne threatening Agnes (Lewes' wife) with the exposure of a previous illegitimate child: 'When she felt herself threatened, Marian could react brutally.' Of the early relationship between Lewes and Marian she remarks that, in addition to their intellectual interests, they also shared 'a common streak of common coarseness, of emotional vulgarity already apparent in George and increasingly in Marian'. Given a different tone, this might possibly represent praise for a greater roundedness in personality than we have been led to believe.

She is also provocative on the early works, and cites – though it indicates her bias – Anne Fremantle's interesting judgment that *Adam Bede* is a cruel book, since Hetty, like other George Eliot heroines, 'suffered retributive justice for Marian Evans' sins'. She reminds us of George Eliot's deliberate lie in 1859, when Lewes wrote 'she authorises me to state, as distinctly as language can do so, that she is not the author of "Adam Bede" '. There is an interesting focus on the resemblance between *Jermola the Potter* and *Silas Marner*, noted much earlier by Mathilde Blind. Eliza Linton is frequently summoned as a biographical witness: Marghanita Laski 'cannot but agree' with her when she says that Lewes' coarseness 'rubbed off' on Marian, and that 'I have never known anyone so purely artificial as George Eliot...never for an instant did she forget her self-created self – never did she throw away the trappings of the airs of the benign Sybil...She was so consciously "George Eliot"...as to make her society a little overwhelming'. This testimony is clearly not impartial, but Miss Laski can be finely deductive, as with *Daniel Deronda*, where she connects Mirah's singing debut with Sally Shilton's as related by Lady Newdegate, and Gwendolen's guilt over not saving Grandcourt with a story by Paul Heyse, whom George Eliot had met in 1858. She also connects Mirah's intention to drown herself with Mary Wollstonecraft's attempted suicide in 1795. And piecing together a number of references though 'it would be going too far to call them evidence' she makes out the case for Marian discovering after Lewes' death, proofs of his infidelity. There is another good piece of detection in the identification of Francis Newdigate with Captain Wybrow in 'Mr Gilfil'. At the end we are left with some admiration for this discovery of fresh material, though Marghanita Laski's obvious lack of sympathy for her subject remains pervasive.

    George Eliot: The Emergent Self (1975) by Ruby Redinger is a psychobiography of compulsive power, though it will not supersede Haight because so much is internalised. It examines George Eliot's personality as it may have been, and Ruby Redinger is throughout persuasive and, I believe, dedicated to her subject. Her perceptive, intuitive approach is only occasionally marred by too great subjectivity. Documentation throughout the study is exemplary: she acknowledges the valuable earlier studies by Blind, Browning and Haldane, as well as using Cross and Haight delicately and intelligently. Her main thesis is that George Eliot had always wanted to write fiction, and that she was awakened to it by 'the subtly continuing, modulating force of her writing present upon her buried past'. Cross' editing of her letters distorted her personality; 'evidence of her past is removed'. Ruby Redinger concentrates on the early works and much on the early life too, with a close analysis of relationships within the Evans family. She notes 'the rarity of a satisfactory mother' among George Eliot's fictional characters (including Dolly Winthrop and Mrs Garth we might ask?), and looks closely at a late poem, 'Self and Life', with its 'remarkable recall of symbiotic love'. The 'Brother and Sister' sonnet sequence receives expansive analysis ('love and fear are also important thematic elements'), and Ruby Redinger believes that by growing into the pseudonym of 'George Eliot' Marian freed her 'second self for writing'. *The Mill* reflects her 'need for justification'. The arguments are closely integrated in reference: a convincing emphasis is maintained. Marian's refusal to attend church is interpreted: 'underlying her rebellion against her spiritual father lay her rebellion against her earthly'. The 'husband' relationship with Sara Hennell is sympathetically probed. The 'calmness' of Marian's experience with Herbert Spencer is recorded, though this epithet hardly seems tenable now after the publication of her impassioned letter to him.

As George Eliot emerges from Marian Evans, Miss Redinger indicates the price she paid for the anguish of creativity. She considers, however, that 'The pseudonym was a synthesising agent in her life', but points to George Eliot's constant illness while writing. She perceptively views *The Mill* as 'an act of confession, not one of mere retaliation'. In her analysis of the early novels she discerns 'dynamic ambivalence' in *Adam Bede*, and she also says that George Eliot is concerned in her work with 'a new breadth of vision', rather than with inculcating or being didactic. The date of 'The Lifted Veil' (1859; set in 1850) is cleverly connected with George Eliot's life at the time. But we have to admit that occasionally Ruby Redinger reveals strain in her determined interpretations. Thus 'The curiously sadistic portrait of Romola was a means of self-flagellation for her creator, who was convinced that she had strayed from her earliest goals, the selfless ones that she forced her heroine to fulfil'.

Ruby Redinger accurately finds a loss of creativity after Lewes' death, asserting, again rightly I believe, 'It was the force of memory that had largely dictated the sequence of her fiction'. She connects Strauss with Casaubon: Strauss said in his *Life of Jesus* 'This is the key to the whole of Christology', and Ruby Redinger observes, 'the Key to all Mythologies is a parody of Strauss' explication'. I doubt it; and there are other dubious emphases (did George Eliot marry Cross to get away from Edith Simcox?). But the overall effect is positive, challenging, new in stance and boldly deductive.

Two feminist critics, Elaine Showalter and Ellen Moers, have made particularly important contributions to George Eliot studies. Elaine Showalter in *A Literature of their Own* (1978) points out that in *Romola* George Eliot poses the question of where 'the duty of obedience ends and the duty of resistance begins'. Her excellent, in-depth study reveals an extensive background of scholarship and wide reading in women's literature (much of it neglected, forgotten or ignored). She quotes the *Saturday Review* in 1860 as observing of *Adam Bede* that 'to speak the simple truth, without affectation or politeness, it was thought to be too good for a woman's story'. Elaine Showalter asserts that George Eliot's superiority depressed her 'female contemporaries'. After investigating a minor novel by Elizabeth Robbins, *George Mandeville's Husband* (1894), a satire on George Eliot, she notes how the great novelist's style permeates that of other writers; 'Eliot's example was as inescapable as it was inimitable'. Of *The Mill* she says that George Eliot 'elevates suffering into a female career…Another important metaphor for Maggie is the gypsy queen, a fantasy that Eliot realistically and humorously undercuts'. She believes that 'Maggie cannot face the truth about her own feelings', and calls Maggie's drifting with Stephen 'colluding in the elopement'. There are other forthright, if questionable, assertions, such as 'Eliot's metaphor for Maggie's evasion of responsibility is opium', and she notes the convincing nature of the portrait of 'Tom Tulliver's emotional petrification'. Space precludes further quotation, but this is an outstanding book which places George Eliot among her contemporary sisterhood and establishes both her distinguished differences and the nature of her kinships.

Ellen Moers' *Literary Women* (1978) is less wide-ranging, though it fulfils its claim to making 'a major contribution to feminist scholarship'. There is an interesting emphasis on Lewes' supportive attitude towards women's literature, and an equally stimulating glance at the influence of Harriet Beecher Stowe's *Dred* on George Eliot. But Ellen Moers' major contribution is perhaps the association she makes between *Emma* (which George Eliot read in 1857) and *Adam Bede*. Her view is that Jane Austen's novel was 'the one that made [George Eliot] a major novelist'. The analysis of analogies and reversals is interesting but not, I think, conclusive. Derivations from George Sand's *La Petite Fadette* are also examined in detail in relation to *The Mill*. Some of the statements are inaccurate, even flippant in tone; for example 'George Eliot lets Gwendolen Harleth get rid of her dreadful husband by pushing him out of a sailboat in the Mediterranean; of course, it all happens offstage – we cannot be sure what really transpires – but the reader is allowed at least to hope that Gwendolen had a share in Grandcourt's drowning'. The myth of Corinne is related to Dorothea who, we are told, is 'an arrogant, selfish, spoiled, rich beauty, she does little but harm in the novel'. Odd as this emphasis is, it at least sets the reader looking again, as does her analysis of imagery which discovers, for example, genital symbolism in the Red Deeps of *The Mill*. Provocative, even outrageous, Moers is a stimulating critic.

One of the main feminist studies from the 1970s and 1980s is unquestionably Sandra Gilbert's and Susan Gubar's *The Madwoman in the Attic* (1979). The interesting early focus here is on one of George Eliot's lesser treated works, 'The Lifted Veil'. The narrator, Latimer, has much in common with his creator – the early death of his mother, being sent away to school, often ill and needing to be loved. The authors assert that 'this story clearly displays Eliot's consciousness of her place in a tradition of female gothic...George Eliot never allows us to depart from Latimer's consciousness'. Most of this seems sufficiently obvious. More interesting is the emphasis on the importance of George Eliot's marriage to Cross eight months before her death, which 'points us to the importance of her insight in the novels into the deeply inbred dependence of women', while her interest in St Theresa and the Virgin Mother reflects 'an attempt to discover a symbol of uniquely female divinity'. The veil itself receives close scrutiny and, since it is always a woman behind the veil, 'she is part of a strong female tradition'. They point out the connection between *Jane Eyre* and 'Mr Gilfil', while *Scenes* in general forecast 'the camouflages of her later fiction'. From *The Mill* to *Deronda* her novels 'still come across as portraits of female destiny'. The animal imagery, which also runs throughout and is associated with the heroines, tells us that in the novels 'the female is closely linked with the forces of nature'. There is some interesting analysis of the Dorothea-Casaubon marriage as Dorothea realises 'how completely textuality has been substituted for sexuality in her married life'.

In her criticism of masculine standards and attitudes George Eliot makes Mr Brooke 'a dark parody of Casaubon'. And, of course, the society in which she lives 'is controlled by men'. The word 'key' in its various usages becomes 'a symbol of acquisitive and reductive monism'. The authors consider that Rosamond is George Eliot's 'most important study of female rebellion'. There is also some astute comment on what her minor characters say, such as Mrs Cadwallader's 'A woman's choice usually means taking the only man she can get'. In the climactic scene of *Middlemarch*, where Dorothea goes to Rosamond, 'Both women seem childish because both have been denied full maturity by their femininity'. And Farebrother's virtues 'are defined by his "feminine" renunciation, his sensitivity and responsibility for a household of single women'. Will is 'radically antipatriarchal', and he displays a 'feminine strength for survival'. The 'key' to George Eliot's heroines is that they are shown to be in 'the entangled threads of renunciation and rage'.

Gillian Beer's *George Eliot* (1986) offers a clear review of feminist criticism of George Eliot, whose central position was 'of immense worth to other women', though she poses a difficulty for feminist critics because she confines her heroines within 'ordinary possibility'. Kate Millett observed of George Eliot that she was 'stuck with the Ruskinian service ethic...the good woman – nurse, guide, mother, adjunct of the race'. But Gillian Beer believes that 'Her courage was silent. It took the form of writing, of private action, not of public campaign'. She was torn between 'The intransigence of Antigone' and 'the passivity of a Madonna'. Her 'key topic is relations between women and men, men and women', and Gillian Beer emphasises that for George Eliot 'Writing as a woman means writing as a human'. There is also a convincing account of George Eliot's acceptance of her sibylline role – 'It exempted her from being part of the world of genetic descent (it freed her from the actuality and the metaphor of motherhood)'.

Gillian Beer looks closely at George Eliot's review of Fredrika Bremer's *Hertha* (see Pinney [1963], p. 334) in which she said that women 'have to prove that they are capable of accurate thought, severe study, and continuous self-command'. In her comments on Miss Bremer and Geraldine Jewsbury she was dealing with problems 'crucial to her own art', i.e., the act of renunciation. She registers the absence in George Eliot's work of 'the study of female friendship'. There is some sensitive analysis of the presentation of Hetty, where 'the male narrator sacrifices her, allowing her to die'. Gillian Beer says that the problem to which George Eliot always returns poses the questions; 'Is the only form of heroism open to women to be martyrdom?' The dark woman represents passion and disruption. Always in Gillian Beer's commentary there is biographical notation: 'Maggie Tulliver drowns alongside Tom. But George Eliot survived after Marian Evans' alienation from her brother – was even born out of that alienation.' And she notes unerringly that at the end of The Mill 'The freedom that Maggie is offered is the removal of choice'. After Maggie, George Eliot's women have to go on living.

From the following novels she considers fathers and mothers, 'natural parents and nurturing parents'. Romola is 'full of the fragmenting and betraying of fathers', and this 'suggests a psychodrama which has to do with the author's own need'. Moving on to Felix Holt she says that 'the horror of Mrs Transome's position is her powerlessness, and her lack (once Harold has usurped her) of proper occupation'. Middlemarch presents current questions involving the women's movement, and the way George Eliot used a double time-scheme is related to this. Rosamond is seen as an entrapped woman.

George Eliot was not, however, a 'radical feminist', but 'What is demonstrable is that she was intimately familiar with the current writing and actions of the women's movement and that in Middlemarch particularly, she brooded on the curtailment of women's lives in terms drawn from the movement and in sympathy with it'. But where did she stand? Gillian Beer says that 'the activity of the writing incarnates human potentiality' i.e., the way ahead lies in finding your own work, as George Eliot herself discovered. The investigation of Daniel Deronda includes a good account of the importance of voice and vocation: she also notes that in that novel 'The brunt of relationship is borne by mothers'. This book, together with her earlier Darwin's Plots (1983), shows her dedication to George Eliot and in critical, scholarly and imaginative terms Gillian Beer's work must rate as among the most important contributions of the 1980s to our understanding and appreciation of George Eliot.

Jennifer Uglow's George Eliot (1987) maintains a balanced, discriminating perspective on her relationship to feminism. George

Eliot can 'never be drawn easily into the feminist net' and she notes that many would accept that, 'far from being feminist,' she was almost repressively conservative, seeming to believe that accepted female values must be preserved despite change. Jennifer Uglow records George Eliot's 'fascinated delight in language' and also the expansiveness of her mind, quoting from the Journal about her Ilfracombe experience: 'I never longed so much to know the names of things as during this visit to Ilfracombe. The desire is part of the tendency that is now constantly growing in me to escape from all vagueness and inaccuracy into the daylight of distinct, vivid ideas' (Letters II, 250-1). They provided her with new insights, and Jennifer Uglow brilliantly suggests that the experience contributed to 'her desire to keep the sense of diversity and individuality without losing a feeling of inter-relatedness of phenomena'. In this way George Eliot's work transcends narrow period interpretations.

Jennifer Uglow deals with the 'Woman Question' of the 1850s. George Eliot had the advantage at the time of moving in liberal circles, where everything to do with women down to 'the oppression of the double sexual standard' was openly debated. She finds George Eliot detached: 'her single wholehearted commitment was to Barbara Leigh-Smith', and she believes that her attitude towards 'organised feminism' was ambivalent, and that she resisted 'any idealisation of women'. While Jennifer Uglow admires the essays, she points out that in those dealing with women there is the impress of 'a persistent intellectual élitism'. This is linked to the novels, where George Eliot separates the extraordinary women from the common run, 'a pattern she continues in the aspiring heroines of her fiction'. But the essay on 'Silly Novels' does stress 'the falseness of female literature' which makes women 'look negligible and even ludicrous'. She spells out the fact that George Eliot's novels 'are the work of a writer who felt that a woman artist had special gifts and special responsibilities. Ironic then, that in 1856, at the start of her bold career, the "strong-minded woman" could only speak out if she was wearing the mask of a man'.

But it is when she takes a close look at George Eliot's practice that Miss Uglow reveals her own intelligent and subtle readings. Of Scenes she says George Eliot turns back to 'the stereotyped literary forms she pretends to eschew...she uses her heroines to

bridge the gulf between the literary and the real worlds'. She finds
that the 'relationship between Tryan and Janet has a suppressed
eroticism which reminds one of Feuerbach's symbolic use of
sexual union as an emblem of spiritual harmony'. She hits the exact
emphasis when she notes that the novels have 'plots based on
literary conventions' which 'are played out against a background
of realistic description'. She believes that Hetty is not punished for
sensuality but for 'compulsive dreaming', and she ponders on the
effect of George Eliot's 'feminised men' and their sympathetic
roles.

When Jennifer Uglow turns to The Mill she finds that the 'rich
imaginations' of Maggie and her father help to 'cause their
downfall'. There is an analysis of the way the novel is 'permeated
with metaphor'. Even more subtle is the suggestion that 'the
dislocated form of the book' approximates to Maggie's 'chaotic
personality, rich in imagination, weak in judgment'. The death of
Maggie and Tom 'is an epiphany'. The structure of Silas Marner,
though, is compared to a 'country dance'. Most interesting is the
Dolly/Silas interaction, at once comic and serious: Silas 'could be
initiated into female mystery', and he even assumes 'the role of the
local Wise Woman'. Miss Uglow notes the irony in the conception
of Romola, the fact that Lewes virtually told George Eliot what to
do here, while the novel is about 'the way a passionate intellectual
woman responds to being told what to do all her life by men'. She
finds Romola George Eliot's 'most striking exposition of the role of
women', a parable of the way Victorian men tried to 'define
women'. Romola's own philanthropy brings her close to Victorian
women such as Florence Nightingale and Octavia Hill: she 'is
roused to a new life in her own right'. Jennifer Uglow picks up a
point made by Rosemary Ashton (1983) that Romola is the one
work of George Eliot's which can carry the label 'positivist'.

She also examines the guiding metaphors of Felix Holt,
analysing that novel's version of 'male hostility towards an unruly,
dangerous element in women which threatens to overturn their
plans'. Middlemarch is permeated by George Eliot's 'feminist
analysis'. There is a sharp look at the influence of the figure of
Antigone, and in considering Dorothea's fate she says of her and
others like her; 'their spirit can be conveyed only through myth and
poetry, the only languages which suggest the true measure of
female power'. In Daniel Deronda she sees a contrast between the

good 'feminine receptivity' of Daniel and the ' "bad" feminine character of Gwendolen'. She says 'The harsh fact is that all women have to sell is themselves', and gambling certainly has worse consequences for a woman than a man. She rightly stresses that 'the portrait of Alchirisi (sic) burns with energy'. It does. The Princess is arguably the most positive feminist in George Eliot's fiction.

Chapter 10
State of the Art: Current Developments

Valentine Cunningham, in *Everywhere Spoken Against: Dissent in the Victorian Novel* (1975) examines in great detail the deep levels at which George Eliot worked in her early fiction. He quotes her own words from the essay on Riehl; 'Why can we not have pictures of religious life among the industrial classes in England, as interesting as Mrs Stowe's pictures of religious life among the negroes?', and also an appreciative commentary on the presentation of Dinah from the *Nonconformist* (16 April 1859); 'The generous spirituality and warm devotion of this simple, grave, loving young Methodist, are represented with a true appreciation and sympathy, which are altogether beautiful and excellent.' That may be so, and Cunningham demonstrates George Eliot's closeness to the text of Southey's *Life of Wesley* in certain instances. He points out that Mr Tryan was 'an ideal character', and does some interesting tracing of Dinah's connection with the real Elizabeth Evans (née Tomlinson). Just as Dinah was apparently able to leave Snowfield at will in order to undertake her preaching, so Elizabeth was so important to her employer at the Nottingham lace factory where she worked that 'he wanted to keep her services, whatever outrageous terms her career as a preacher dictated'.

There is considerable research too on the character of the Dissenting minister, Rufus Lyon, in *Felix Holt*. Cunningham concludes that 'despite the accuracy, the sympathy, and the minimal caricature, Rufus Lyon is unsatisfactory'. The original is obviously the father of the Misses Franklin, whose school Marian Evans attended. He was minister of the Cow Lane Baptist Chapel from 1798-1852. This was in Coventry, and Cunningham notes further that 'the industries of Treby Magna, tape-weaving and watch-making, were Coventry trades'. Felix is a watch-maker, and this 'allows him to work at home and therefore (good humanist) teach boys as he works'. Cunningham establishes a strong series of identification marks between the Treby Magna of the novel and the Coventry of fact. Altogether, it is an impressive piece of research on the careful documentation George Eliot undertook to get her facts, to get the 'medium' in which her religious characters moved, absolutely right. His concluding paragraph on her achievement is a warm tribute: 'No great English novelist has got closer than George Eliot to the heart of the Dissenting matter.'

Neil Roberts' *George Eliot: Her Beliefs and Her Art* (1975) is a competent and at times stimulating introduction to the novels. One of his key themes is 'complexity': 'the characteristic form of her novels is a complex organisation of the cause and effect of moral action'; and 'reality must be treated in its fullest complexity'. Another key word is 'sympathy', which, he perceptively notes, was 'first learned from Wordsworth before she found it confirmed in Comte and Feuerbach'. Roberts indicates the importance of Comte in George Eliot's development as he sees it, believing that she absorbed his ideas. He bases his view on the way Comte satisfied her 'intellectual and emotional nature by simultaneously providing (in her view) a more objective basis for morality and showing it to be dependent on the reverence for the past which was part of her own moral nature'. Feeling is also given predominance over intellect in George Eliot's development.

With Feuerbach the object of reverence was Humanity, as distinct from the individual of the species. Roberts, like so many of George Eliot's critics, believes that her conservatism increased with the years. He also says, and I am sure he is right, that 'lying deeper than any theories about society, there is an intensely strong feeling about her personal past, which becomes part and parcel of the sense of the social and natural past'. Other stimulating emphases are given when he examines the result of the 'egoist's "will"…set against a clearly inevitable sequence of events'. Moreover, there is a succinct tracing of evolutionary ideas on her writing. Innate moral qualities are derived from the example of ancestors: in George Eliot's fiction, the 'sanctity of the past is the most frequent and damaging source of didacticism'. 'Janet's Repentance' is her 'first fully characteristic work', while in *Adam Bede* she 'creates the illusion of a stable and immemorial rural world'.

Roberts draws an interesting analogy between the brother/sister relationship in *The Mill* and that in Dickens' *Our Mutual Friend*, though in the former he finds that the didacticism 'falsifies the drama'. In *Romola* 'didacticism triumphs completely over imagination'. In *Felix Holt* he considers there to be a failure in social analysis. His focus on *Middlemarch* is on its overwhelming sense of reality and its 'depressing sense of a deterministic process quenching effort and aspiration'. We 'experience history as it was experienced by the obscure inhabitants of a provincial town'. He says – and there is a neat truth in the analogy – that Ladislaw 'might be called George Eliot's Scholar-Gypsy'. Roberts' analysis of *Daniel Deronda* is especially interesting: he believes it to be 'a magnificent achievement, possibly surpassing even *Middlemarch*', and he draws special attention to the highly original nature of the opening and the conclusion, though what he says about the gambling motif and the necklace sequence has, I think, been fully explored elsewhere (see for example, Barbara Hardy). His appraisal of Gwendolen's sexuality is excellent.

Robert Liddell reveals in *The Novels of George Eliot* (1977) that he was invited to write the book, and this shows. He looks closely at George Eliot's puritanism, and finds it responsible for her didacticism. He also says accusingly that George Eliot 'sometimes tries to create a moral conflict where there is none'. Liddell demonstrates through close attention to character that she appreciated Casuistry. He criticises her philistinism, but finds the pathos of 'Amos' genuine. He unerringly picks out the weak point of Tryan being given 'a sin in the past to expiate'. In the *Scenes* he selects for notice the sentimental treatment of the heroines, and boldly asserts that 'George Eliot's children are always badly done': it is the humour in her early works which 'gives the best promise of what is to come'.

Liddell seems to be intent on revaluing the revaluation of George Eliot. He tells us that 'We owe a debt of gratitude to the first readers of the *Scenes* who so greatly over-rated them. But for their excessive praise George Eliot would have been discouraged, and we might have had no more fiction from her!' Although he has defended the use of plot summary in criticism (1977) pp. 9-10, there is far too much of it in this book. At the same time Liddell picks out her 'characteristic device of prophecy', though asserting, I think rightly, that the 'breath of cows and the scent of hay' which she advertised in *Adam Bede* are not as 'omnipresent' as she implied. He finds that the main faults in *The Mill* largely derive from a too strong authorial identification with Maggie, while the final reconciliation is 'a kind of wish fulfilment'. One of his favourite anti-themes is developed: 'George Eliot never had any idea how to make children speak'; though he substitutes the word 'fun' for the often used word about the early work, 'charm', observing of the latter that George Eliot is totally devoid of it. In *The Mill* he praises the salesmanship of Mr Riley and Bob Jakin, and when he turns to *Silas Marner* he commends the narrative role of Mr Macey. *Romola*, as we might expect, comes in for a severe attack: 'Tito and Romola are overwhelmed, like guests of small account, who have the misfortune to attend a party too grand for them.' Here the summary is even more profuse, though the nature of Tito's temptation is given positive attention. *Felix Holt* 'is a new beginning, and a different kind of failure', and already Liddell is looking ahead to 'the flatulent imagery of *Middlemarch*'. Of the Transome estate complexities he accuses George Eliot of creating 'the minimum of interest from the maximum of obscurity': he certainly has a point. Of Felix he says 'He is not the Warwickshire working-man, so well-known to George Eliot, but a carefully excogitated urban working-man, whose voice she could never have heard except in fantasy'. He cites George Eliot's famous statement that there is no private life which is not conditioned by the wider public life, and then refutes it with reference to the isolation of the Jermyn-Mrs Transome story.

Middlemarch is praised for the fact that 'each of the main characters is very much more than a character; he is an embodiment of an important theme in the book'. Obsessed by Casaubon, Liddell summarises the relevant parts of the plot: but he picks out Harriet Bulstrode for special mention, just as Joan Bennett (1948) had done. And he says 'Middlemarch itself, with its county surroundings at Freshitt, Tipton and Lowick, is the real subject of the book'. He goes on; 'The best talk is often that of the lighter characters'. As if caught in the act of overpraising, Liddell then adjusts his stance: according to him, the 'web' image is overdone, much of the imagery 'verges on the grotesque', and the 'scientific metaphors are no happier'. All in all, this means that 'The book is disfigured by a quantity of references and quotations of an oddness or pretentiousness which perhaps originate in the author's autodidacticism; she never learned the art of literary tact which avoids them'.

After he has produced 'A Table of Kindred and Affinity in

Middlemarch' he proceeds to discuss at some length the parallels between *Daniel Deronda* and James' *Portrait of a Lady*, already adequately undertaken by Leavis (1948). After saying that George Eliot insisted on 'the double standard' and that Romola is 'enskyed and sainted' he asserts that 'the subsequent revaluation of George Eliot has gone too far – and when we are asked to admire the "archness" of Mary Garth or the "venturesome lightness" of Gwendolen Harleth more than the brilliance of Millamant, we can be very sure that the author's reputation is due for another slump'. She is 'a most imperfect artist', who 'commands our admiration', though we cannot give her our affection. And he admits, as if we didn't know, that 'one of the aims of this book is a protective and partial depreciation – a jettisoning of false and exaggerated claims, and an admission of weaknesses'.

Some of Liddell's assertions suggest that, for him, the clock stopped somewhere around 1948. His is a curious mixture of rambling generalisations and astute focal points of evaluation, but, even so, a bold book. Since 1959 the tide in George Eliot studies appears to have flowed all one way, and I sometimes feel that searching investigation is carried out where it is hardly worth the trouble. Felicia Bonaparte's *The Triptych and the Cross: The Central Myths of George Eliot's Poetic Imagination* (1979) is as weighed down with learning as is *Romola* itself. The Introduction makes some curious judgments: *Felix Holt* is 'a tangled political melodrama' and *Silas Marner* 'a work of uncertain form and dubious perspective'. This naturally leads to an even more tangled work of uncertain form and deliberate perspective, namely *Romola*. Felicia Bonaparte says that readers have not recognised 'the relationship between realism and poetry in George Eliot's work'. For her *Romola* is not just a poetic novel; it is a complete poem, and as such, 'It is a landmark in the development of the novel'. The broad outlines are easily clarified: Bacchus versus Christ; Tito versus Dino (and Savonarola): Romola represents Antigone and Alcestis (here Tito is Admetus). But although Felicia Bonaparte is interesting, particularly on the 'turning point' year of 1492, we wonder whether this examination will win new readers for *Romola*, or merely new scholars intent on subterranean explication.

Rosemary Ashton's *George Eliot* (1983) in the Past Masters series is an admirable, succinct introduction, with a sure summary of the influences which shaped George Eliot in her early years and in the formative period of her life as translator and journalist. Rosemary Ashton is immersed in her subject, and points are made clearly and independently, with an easy narrative verve. She is particularly good on the scientific study of provincial life, *The Spanish Gypsy* and *Daniel Deronda*. Her conclusions always rest on sound and sometimes inspirational investigation, as when she alerts the reader to the time-analogy betweeen *The Winter's Tale* and *Silas Marner*. The quality of her insight comes through in such statements as; 'If in her philosophy George Eliot combined a general optimism with a specific pessimism, in her political views she embraced both approval of radical progress and reluctance to see traditions change.' This observation does not, however, prevent George Eliot from transcending her time in a number of ways, not least being her comparatively open treatment of sexual relationships. Rosemary Ashton neatly puts down W.E. Henley's wisecracks about George Eliot (he called her 'George Sand *plus* Science and *minus* Sex' and 'Pallas with prejudices and a corset') by asserting 'Sexuality was a subject she handled unsensationally and uncoyly, as an integral part of the lives of individuals'. It is an important index to the nature of George Eliot's achievement.

Gillian Beer's *Darwin's Plots* (1983) is a distinguished work of interrelated literary, scientific and philosophical scholarship. For the student of George Eliot and Thomas Hardy it must rank as one of the most important books of recent times. It is almost as necessary to the practice of informed criticism of 19th-century fiction as Darwin's *Origin of Species* was to science. As Gillian Beer says, 'reading *The Origin* is an act which involves you in a narrative experience' and it is her own ability to relate scientific theory to narrative practice which makes *Darwin's Plots* compelling narrative in its own right. For the general reader, the first part, with its readily understood analogies, works best. For instance, she compares the influence of Darwin on his own time to the influence of Freud on ours. Further, she notes that 'evolutionary theory is first a form of imaginative history'. Her analysis of Darwin's language, the influence of the 'immensity of his unguarded reading', is superb. When she turns to *Middlemarch* and *Daniel Deronda*, she provides vital instances of how George Eliot absorbed and responded to Darwin's theories.

Darwin's langugage virtually provided an extension of the

language of fiction. Gillian Beer observes that 'diversification, not truth to type, is the creative principle', and George Eliot extended her own extensive range by acquiring 'the cultural language of science'. George Eliot's own researches on Lydgate indicate her capacity for extension from a given point of discovery, and although she was initially troubled by some of Darwin's ideas – she did not immediately grasp his fundamental concept of natural selection – she makes Mr Brooke say of science that 'it leads to everything'. Gillian Beer rightly italicises this apparently casual remark from a character who is an inveterate dabbler and meddler. That she does so is important to our appreciation of her work, as well as Darwin's and George Eliot's. In her letters and fiction George Eliot did not write at any length about Darwin, but just as his science was literature so, I think it can be truthfully said, her literature, particularly in her last two novels, was science. This integration and diversification was one of her greatest achievements. *Darwin's Plots* examines the 'evolution' of narrative extension from scientific theory, and makes for an investigation that is scientific and historical, creative and scholarly, and throughout imaginative.

George Eliot and Blackmail (1985) by Alexander Welsh is an ingenious and brilliant study. Good criticism should provide refreshment: this is a banquet. After the definitions of blackmail – interesting and far-reaching in themselves – there is a detailed examination of Hitchcock's 1929 film *Blackmail* followed by Miss Braddon's sensational novel, *Lady Audley's Secret*. These preambles to George Eliot are essential reading: Welsh demonstrates the ways in which she used the common sensational material of her lesser contemporaries in her own novels. There is a clever examination of George Eliot's life and the blackmail situations inherent in it, for example her own unmarried status or Liggins' claim to have written *Scenes* and *Adam Bede*. Another interesting focus is on the 'sportive' blackmail in 'Brother Jacob'. *Romola* receives sensitive treatment: Welsh rightly says that it 'is not merely an interruption in the series of novels about English life', but that its writing, with its new perspectives, was productive of the novels to come. These are 'much more efforts of representation than projection'. The section headed 'Murdering Grandcourt' is an impressive exposition of the blackmail theme and its complexities. The final chapter of this important book looks at Hawthorne's *The*

Scarlet Letter and Dickens' *Bleak House* in passing in relation to Freud. The range is impressive, the linking with George Eliot definitive. Here is 'a new searching light', to appropriate her phrase, shed on her art.

In *George Eliot and Nineteenth Century Science* (1984) Sally Shuttleworth is firmly anchored in the theoretical thought of the period. She underlines much of what had already been discerned, though not fully explored, that is, the extent of George Eliot's scientific interests and how she integrated them into her work. Sally Shuttleworth notes that George Eliot's knowledge of science was 'unmatched by any of her peers'. The centre of her own study is 'the field of organic theory', and in her structure she follows George Eliot's own 'pattern of composition'. She records the changes and developments in George Eliot's scientific thought from *Adam Bede* onwards and examines the common belief, which she shared with Comte, Lewes and Herbert Spencer, 'that science could provide the foundations for a system of ethical conduct'. In *Adam Bede* the harvest supper is 'a celebration of historical stasis and simultaneous recognition of evolutionary progress'. In *The Mill* she records the narrator's 'Proust-like submergence into the world of unconscious memory'. In *Silas Marner* Silas' repetitive activity shows George Eliot employing the 'physiological theory', while in *Romola* Savonarola appears to preach 'the positivist doctrine of altruism outlined by Comte'. There is an interesting focus on the then popular 'science' of phrenology in *Felix Holt*, as well as a continuing appraisal of Comte, whose approach to history posits that 'social change is represented primarily in terms of mental development'. In *Middlemarch* she notes the constant shifts in perspective within the chapters and which reflect the mixed nature 'of the social organism itself'. In *Daniel Deronda* George Eliot adopted 'a more open narrative form than in her earlier work'. The 'variety of narrative strategies' which Sally Shuttleworth's analysis of the novels reveals is abundantly, incisively clear. Another piece in the jig-saw of George Eliot's intellectual life is fitted in here.

Two other books, a decade apart but both related, and both essential reading, are Hugh Witemeyer's *George Eliot and the Visual Arts* (1979) and Beryl Gray's *George Eliot and Music* (1989). The first expands on the fact that George Eliot was a 'devoted student of pictures during her thirty years in London'. Witemeyer points out that she had an amazing visual memory and traces connections between portraiture and character in her work. Witemeyer's range matches his subject, and he notes that when she compares Ladislaw to a Royalist, we are at once reminded that 'Dorothea is a Puritan', with all the contrast and complexity which that implies. He also explores the various aspects of George Eliot's landscape vision, and notes that her novels 'abound with picturesque descriptions in an 18th-century vein'. There is a high incidence of landscape description in the *Letters*. George Eliot, as we might expect, has special affinities with 'pretty bits of Midland landscape'. Witemeyer also records the presence of the country-house portrait in her works, giving most prominence to the 'neo-Gothic Cheverel Manor'. He underlines the influence of Ruskin and the pre-Raphaelite painters, while of her time in Ilfracombe with Lewes in 1856 he says that 'Art and science were in perfect harmony during these happy months'. The widespread influence of the visual arts in her work is undeniable: 'In natural description, then in characterisation and domestic scenes, George Eliot was deeply influenced by pictorial conventions.'

Beryl Gray's fascinating book investigates how music permeates both George Eliot's life and her writings. She believes that music 'arches over' her work and 'greatly illuminates her artistry'. In a persuasive biographical section she praises the Brays for extending the young Marian Evans' capacity for appreciation, so that 'her sententiousness yielded to musical exuberance'. She then looks at Marian's encounter with the cosmopolitan culture of Geneva, followed by the quick acquisition of a piano when she lodged with Chapman. She attended Covent Garden regularly with Herbert Spencer. Music had become and continued to be 'an integral part of her domestic life, and fundamental to her social relationships'.

Over half the book is devoted to an investigation of *The Mill*. As Beryl Gray says, 'it is with Maggie Tulliver that George Eliot first fully shares her own capacity for musical absorption'. The effect of sound in the novel is tellingly indicated; and in a sense, for Beryl Gray sub-text becomes sound-text. She notes George Eliot's exactitude of musical choice, the care with which she worked out exchanges and emphases, going to the manuscript of *The Mill* to substantiate her conclusions. 'Stephen's vocal imperfections' are stressed; Philip's choice of song shows his 'connectedness' with

Maggie's childhood, the poignancy deriving from the fact that it celebrates 'perfect sexual love'. In *Middlemarch* she finds that 'music and musical allusion codify and stratify the fictive world, and reveal the capacity for sympathy of each principal character'. In a penetrating appraisal she singles out the weaknesses which undermine the reality of Ladislaw. Despite all his singing, we never *hear* him, 'the register of his voice is never given'. The changing role of music in the Lydgate-Rosamond relationship is carefully analysed, and there is a beautiful focus on 'The self-revealing power of Dorothea's voice'. *Daniel Deronda* marks the full maturity of musical influence and its expression. Here some independent interpretations are backed by a scholarly investigation of George Eliot's debts to the Belgian musical historian Fetis and Hulla's *History of Modern Music*. Though in terms of its own structure the chapter on *The Mill* is perhaps over-long (and there is some straying from the muscial to the peripherally aural), this study researches new areas of George Eliot's art with marked success.

Conclusion

Writing about George Levine's recent bibliography of George Eliot (1988), Joseph Wiesenfarth, himself a distinguished George Eliot critic and scholar, states that it 'reminds us once again of those to whom we are most in debt: the late Gordon S. Haight, the late W.J. Harvey, David R. Carroll, Jerome Beaty, Barbara Hardy, and U.C. Knoepflmacher'. I hope that the necessarily brief coverage of their work provided here will acknowledge this and perhaps add a few more names. It is difficult to forecast exactly what will happen in George Eliot studies, but perhaps safe to say that a fall in critical interest or the status accorded her work is unlikely in the foreseeable future. The Pratt-Neufeld edition of *George Eliot's 'Middlemarch' Notebooks* (1979) 'completes the study begun by Anna T. Kitchel and Jerome Beaty of the evolution of *Middlemarch*': there seems little doubt that gaps elsewhere will continue to be filled. As U.C. Knoepflmacher pointed out, 'more was written on George Eliot from 1960 to 1974 than in the entire century between the appearance of *Adam Bede* in 1859 and the publication of the books by Jerome Thale, Barbara Hardy and Reva Stump in 1959'. And I suspect that between 1974 and 1989 the increase has been even greater, with the absorption of such critical disciplines as structuralism and deconstruction. Kathleen Adams, in *Those of Us Who Loved Her* (1980), has written about the men in George Eliot's life. The Brays and Hennells and Herbert Spencer can expect more extended treatment. Rosemary Ashton's forthcoming biography of Lewes will shed further light both on George Eliot and on her relationship to him. The Clarendon edition of her works will be completed, the manuscripts and notebooks yielding up their related detail. If Edith Simcox is regarded as important, then we can expect Mrs Congreve, Elma Stuart and others of George Eliot's circle to provide scholarly (or other) writers with the opportunity of adding their mite to the store of George Eliot studies. There remains, however, one major gap. What the biographer Richard Ellmann did for Joyce and Wilde needs to be done for George Eliot. In post-Redinger biographical approaches to her there is only failure and distortion. Ina Taylor (1989) hasn't even the merit of being entertaining, unlike Terence de Vere White's *Johnnie Cross* (1983), a subtly suggestive novel about George Eliot's 'widow'. Haight's is the great factual biography, but the critical biography, connecting the life more intimately with the art, has yet to be written.

Bibliography

This is divided as follows:

A. Works by George Eliot.
B. Critical bibliography.

Cross references are marked*

A. Works by George Eliot:

Fiction and poetry: details of first publication

Scenes of Clerical Life (*Blackwood's Magazine*, Jan.-Nov. 1857)
'The Lifted Veil' (*Blackwood's Magazine*, July 1859)
Adam Bede, 3 vols (William Blackwood and Sons, 1859)
The Mill on the Floss, 3 vols (William Blackwood and Sons, 1860)
Silas Marner: The Weaver of Raveloe (William Blackwood and Sons, 1861)
Romola (*Cornhill Magazine*, July 1862-August 1863)
'Brother Jacob' (*Cornhill Magazine*, July 1864)
Felix Holt: The Radical, 3 vols (William Blackwood and Sons, 1866)
The Spanish Gypsy (William Blackwood and Sons, 1868)
Middlemarch: A Study of Provincial Life (William Blackwood and Sons, Dec. 1871-Dec. 1872) [issued in eight parts]
The Legend of Jubal and Other Poems (William Blackwood and Sons, 1874)
Daniel Deronda (William Blackwood and Sons, Feb.- Sept. 1876) [issued in eight parts]
Impressions of Theophrastus Such (William Blackwood and Sons, 1879)

Translations

The Life of Jesus Critically Examined, by D. Strauss (Chapman Brothers, 1846)
The Essence of Christianity, by L. Feuerbach (John Chapman, 1854)

Essays

Essays and Leaves from a Notebook (William Blackwood and Sons, 1884)
Early Essays (Westminster Press, 1919)
The Essays of George Eliot, ed. T. Pinney (Routledge and Kegan Paul, 1963)

Letters

The George Eliot Letters, 9 vols, ed. G.S. Haight (USA: Yale University Press; UK: Oxford University Press, 1954-78)

Annotated Editions

The Penguin English Library (1965-80)
The Clarendon Edition of the Novels of George Eliot (1980-)

B. Critical bibliography

Adam, I., 'Character and Destiny in George Eliot's Fiction', *Nineteenth-Century Fiction* 20 (1965), pp. 127-43
—— 'The Structure of Realisms in *Adam Bede*', *Nineteenth-Century Fiction* 30 (1975), pp. 127-49
—— (ed.), *This Particular Web* (University of Toronto Press, 1975)
Adams, K., *Those of Us Who Loved Her* (George Eliot Fellowship, 1980)
Allen, W., *George Eliot* (USA: Macmillan; UK: Weidenfeld and Nicolson, 1964)
Allott, M., 'George Eliot in the 1860s', *Victorian Studies* 5 (1961), pp. 93-108
Ashton, R., *The German Idea: Four English Writers and the Reception of German Thought, 1800-1860* (Cambridge University Press, 1980)
—— *George Eliot* (Oxford University Press, 1983)
Auerbach, N., 'The Power of Hunger: Demonism and Maggie Tulliver', *Nineteenth-Century Fiction* 30 (1975), pp. 150-71
Auster, H., *Local Habitations: Regionalism in the Early Novels of George Eliot* (Harvard University Press, 1970)
Axon, W.E.A., *English Dialect Society Miscellanies* (1880)
Baker, W., *George Eliot and Judaism*, Salzburg Studies in English Literature (Institut für Englische Sprache und Literatur, University of Salzburg, 1975)
—— (ed.), *Some George Eliot Notebooks: An Edition of the Carl*

*H. Pforzheimer Library's George Eliot Holograph Notebooks,
707, 708, 709, 710, 711* (Institut für Englische Sprache und
Literatur, University of Salzburg, 1976-85)

Bamber, L., 'Self-Defeating Politics in George Eliot's *Felix Holt',
Victorian Studies* 18 (1975), pp. 419-35

Beaty, J., 'History by Indirection: The Era of Reform in *Middlemarch', Victorian Studies* 1 (1958), pp. 173-9

—— 'The Forgotten Past of Will Ladislaw', *Nineteenth-Century
Fiction* 13 (1958), pp. 159-63

—— *Middlemarch: From Notebook to Novel: A Study of George
Eliot's Creative Method* (University of Illinois Press, 1960)

Beebe, M., 'Visions are Creators: the Unity of *Daniel Deronda*',
Boston University Studies in English 1 (1955), pp. 166-77

Beer, G., 'Beyond Determinism: George Eliot and Virginia Woolf',
in *Jacobus, M. (1979), pp. 80-99

—— *Darwin's Plots: Evolutionary Narrative in Darwin, George
Eliot, and Nineteenth-Century Fiction* (Routledge and Kegan
Paul, 1983)

—— *George Eliot* (Harvester Press, 1986)

Beer, P., 'Reader, I Married Him': A Study of the Women
Characters in Jane Austen, Charlotte Brontë, Elizabeth Gaskell
and George Eliot* (Macmillan, 1974)

Bennett, J., *George Eliot: Her Mind and Her Art* (Cambridge
University Press, 1948)

Bissell, C.T., 'Social Analysis in the Novels of George Eliot',
English Literary History 8 (1951), pp. 221-39

Blake, K., '*Middlemarch* and the Woman Question', *Nineteenth-
Century Fiction* 31 (1976), pp. 285-312

Blind, M., *George Eliot* (W.H. Allen, 1883)

Bonaparte, F., *Will and Destiny: Morality and Tragedy in George
Eliot's Novels* (New York University Press, 1975)

—— *The Tryptich and the Cross: The Central Myths of George
Eliot's Poetic Imagination* (Harvester Press, 1979)

Bonnell, H.H., *Charlotte Brontë, George Eliot and Jane Austen:
Studies in their Works* (Longman and Company, 1902)

Bourl'honne, P., *Essai de bibliographie intellectuelle et morale,
1819-54* (Librairie Ancienne Honore Champion, 1933)

Brown, J.C., *The Ethics of George Eliot's Works* (William
Blackwood and Sons, 1879)

Brownell, W.C., *Victorian Prose Masters* (Scribners, 1901)

Browning, O., *Life of George Eliot* (Walter Scott, 1890)

Bullen, J.B., 'George Eliot's *Romola* as a Positivist Allegory',
Review of English Studies 26 (1975), pp. 425-35

Bullett, G., *George Eliot: Her Life and Books* (Collins, 1947)

Calder, J., *Women and Marriage in Victorian Fiction* (Thames and Hudson, 1976)

Carroll, D., 'Unity through Analogy: An Interpretation of *Middlemarch*', *Victorian Studies* 2 (1959), pp. 305-16

—— 'The Unity of *Daniel Deronda*', *Essays in Criticism* 9 (1959), pp. 369-80

—— 'An Image of Disenchantment in the Novels of George Eliot', *Review of English Studies* 11 (1960), pp. 29-41

—— '*Felix Holt*: Society as Protagonist', *Nineteenth-Century Fiction* 17 (1962), pp. 237-52

—— '*Silas Marner*: Reversing the Oracles of Religion', *Literary Monographs* 1 (1967), pp. 167-200, 312-14

—— (ed.), *George Eliot: The Critical Heritage* (Routledge and Kegan Paul, 1971) [Superb introduction followed by 69 reviews and overviews of George Eliot's works by her contemporaries]

—— 'The Sybil of Mercia', *Studies in the Novel* 15 (1983), pp. 10-23

Cazamian, M.L., *Le Roman et les idées en Angleterre: L'Influence de la science (1860-1890)* (France: Librairie Istra, 1923), pp. 92-171

Cecil, D., *Early Victorian Novelists: Essays in Revaluation* (Constable, 1934), pp. 309-36

Chase, C., 'The Decomposition of the Elephants: Double-Reading *Daniel Deronda*', *Proceedings of the Modern Language Association* 93 (1978), pp. 215-27

Cockshut, A.O.J., *The Unbelievers: English Agnostic Thought, 1840-1890* (Collins, 1964), pp. 44-58

Cooke, G.W., *George Eliot: A Critical Study* (London, 1883)

Cooper, L., *George Eliot: Writers and Their Works* (published for the British Council by Longmans, 1951)

Creeger, G.R., *George Eliot: A Collection of Critical Essays* (Prentice-Hall, 1970) [Includes essays by Hardy, Pinney, Levine and Carroll, as well as James' '*Daniel Deronda*: A Conversation']

Cross, J.W., *George Eliot's Life as Related in her Letters and Journals*, 3 vols (William Blackwood and Sons, 1885)

Cunningham, V., *Everywhere Spoken Against: Dissent in the Victorian Novel* (Clarendon Press, 1975), pp. 143-89

Daiches, D., *George Eliot: Middlemarch* (Edward Arnold, 1963)

Dawson, W.J., *The Makers of English Fiction*, iii of *The Makers of Modern English* (Hodder and Stoughton, 1899-1905)

Deakin, M., *The Early Life of George Eliot* (Manchester University Press, 1913)

Dowden, E., '*Middlemarch* and *Daniel Deronda*', *Studies in

Literature 1789-1877 (Kegan Paul, 1879), pp. 85-121

Ellmann, R., 'Dorothea's Husbands: Some Biographical Speculations', *Golden Codgers: Biographical Speculations* (Oxford University Press, 1973), pp. 17-38

Elton, O., *A Survey of English Literature 1830-80* (Edward Arnold, 1920)

Fremantle, A., *George Eliot* (Duckworth, 1933)

Gardner, C., *The Inner Life of George Eliot* (Sir Isaac Pitman and Sons, 1912)

Gilbert, S. and Gubar, S., *The Madwoman in the Attic: The Woman Writer and the Nineteenth-Century Literary Imagination* (Yale University Press, 1979)

Gray, B,M., 'Pseudoscience and George Eliot's *The Lifted Veil*', *Nineteenth-Century Fiction* 36 (1982), pp. 407-23

—— *George Eliot and Music* (Macmillan, 1989)

Hagan, J., '*Middlemarch*: Narrative Unity in the Story of Dorothea Brooke', *Nineteenth-Century Fiction* 16 (1961), pp. 17-32

—— 'A Reinterpretation of *The Mill on the Floss*', *Proceedings of the Modern Language Association* 87 (1972), pp. 53-63

Haight, G.S., *George Eliot and John Chapman: With Chapman's Diaries* (Yale University Press, 1940)

—— (ed.), *The George Eliot Letters,* 9 vols (Yale University Press, 1954-78)

—— (ed.), *A Century of George Eliot Criticism* (Methuen, 1966)

—— *George Eliot: A Biography* (Oxford University Press, 1968)

—— and van Asdel (eds), *George Eliot: A Centenary Tribute* (UK: Macmillan; USA: Barnes and Noble, 1982)

—— *Selections from George Eliot's Letters* (Yale University Press, 1985)

Hands, T., *A George Eliot Chronology* (Macmillan Press, 1989)

Hanson, L. and Hanson, E., *Marian Evans and George Eliot* (Oxford University Press, 1952)

Haldane, E.S., *George Eliot and her Times: A Victorian Study* (Hodder and Stoughton, 1927)

Hardy, B., *The Novels of George Eliot: A Study in Form* (Athlone Press, 1959)

—— 'Implication and Incompleteness: George Eliot's *Middlemarch*', *The Appropriate Form: An Essay on the Novel* (Athlone Press, 1964), pp. 105-31

—— (ed.), *Middlemarch: Critical Approaches to the Novel* (Athlone Press, 1967)

—— (ed.), *Critical Essays on George Eliot* (Routledge and Kegan Paul, 1970)

—— 'Middlemarch: Public and Private Worlds', English 25 (1976), pp. 5-26

—— Particularities: Readings in George Eliot (Peter Owen, 1982)

—— 'George Eliot', Forms of Feeling in Victorian Fiction (Methuen, 1985), pp. 131-57

Harvey, W.J., The Art of George Eliot (Chatto and Windus, 1961)

Holloway, J., The Victorian Sage: Studies in Argument (St Martin's Press, 1953), pp. 11-57

Holmstrom, J. and Lerner, L. (eds), George Eliot and her Readers: A Selection of Contemporary Reviews (The Bodley Head, 1966)

Hussey, M., 'Structure and Imagery in Adam Bede', Nineteenth-Century Fiction 10 (1955), pp. 115-29

Hutton, R.H., Essays on Some of the Modern Guides of English Thought in Matters of Faith (Macmillan, 1887), pp. 145-300

—— A Victorian Spectator, Tener, R. and Woodfield, M. (eds), (The Bristol Press, 1989)

Jacobus, M. (ed.), Women Writing about Women (UK: Croom Helm; USA: Barnes & Noble, 1979)

—— 'The Question of Language: Men of Maxims and The Mill on the Floss', Critical Inquiry 8 (1981), pp. 207-22

James, H., 'The Novels of George Eliot', Atlantic Monthly 18 (1866), pp. 479-92

—— 'The Spanish Gypsy', North American Review 107 (1868), pp. 620-35

—— Review of Middlemarch, Galaxy 15 (1873), pp. 424-8

—— 'Daniel Deronda: A Conversation', Atlantic Monthly 38 (1876), pp. 684-94

Kaufman, D., George Eliot and Judaism: An Attempt to Appreciate 'Daniel Deronda', trans. from the German by Ferrier, J.W. (William Blackwood and Sons, 1877)

Kettle, A., An Introduction to the English Novel: From Defoe to George Eliot (Hutchinson, 1951), pp. 171-90

Kitchel, A.T., George Lewes and George Eliot: A Review of Records (The John Day Company, 1933)

Knoepflmacher, U.C., Religious Humanism and the Victorian Novel: George Eliot, Walter Pater, and Samuel Butler (Princeton University Press, 1965), pp. 24-148

—— George Eliot's Early Novels: The Limits of Realism (University of California Press, 1968)

—— 'Middlemarch: Affirmation through Compromise', Laughter and Despair: Readings in Ten Novels of the Victorian Era (University of California Press, 1971), pp. 109-35

—— 'Middlemarch: An Avuncular View', Nineteenth-Century

Fiction 30 (1975), pp. 53-81

—— and Levine, G., 'George Eliot', *Nineteenth-Century Fiction* 35 (1980) [*special issue*: 'George Eliot 1880-1980']

Laski, M., *George Eliot and Her World* (Thames and Hudson, 1973)

Leavis, F.R., *The Great Tradition* (Chatto and Windus, 1948), pp. 28-125

—— 'George Eliot's Zionist Novel', *Commentary* 30 (1960), pp. 317-25

—— Intro. to *Daniel Deronda* (Harper Torchbook, 1960)

Lerner, L., *The Truthtellers: Jane Austen, George Eliot, D.H. Lawrence* (Chatto and Windus, 1967), pp. 235-78

Levenson, S.F., 'The Use of Music in *Daniel Deronda*', *Nineteenth-Century Fiction* 24 (1969), pp. 317-34

Levine, G., 'Determinism and Responsibility in the Works of George Eliot', *Proceedings of the Modern Language Association* 77 (1962), pp. 268-79

—— 'Isabel, Gwendolen and Dorothea', *English Literary History* 30 (1963), pp. 244-57

—— 'George Eliot's Hypothesis of Reality', *Nineteenth-Century Fiction* 35 (1980), pp. 1-28

—— *The Realistic Imagination: English Fiction from Frankenstein to Lady Chatterley* (University of Chicago Press, 1981), pp. 252-316

—— *An Annotated Bibliography of George Eliot* (Harvester Press, 1988)

Liddell, R., *The Novels of George Eliot* (Duckworth, 1977)

Linton, E.L., *My Literary Life* (Hodder and Stoughton, 1899)

Lisle, B.J., 'Art and Egoism in George Eliot's Poetry', *Victorian Poetry* 22 (1984), pp. 263-78

May, J.L., *George Eliot: A Study* (Cassell, 1930)

McKenzie, K.A., *Edith Simcox and George Eliot* (Oxford University Press, 1961)

McSweeney, K., *Middlemarch* (Allen and Unwin, 1984)

Miller, J.H., *The Forms of Victorian Fiction: Thackeray, Dickens, Trollope, George Eliot, Meredith, and Hardy* (University of Notre Dame Press, 1968)

—— 'Narrative and History', *English Literary History* 41 (1974), pp. 455-73

Millett, K., *Sexual Politics* (Abacus, 1972)

Moers, E., *Literary Women* (Doubleday, 1976)

Mottram, W., *The True Story of George Eliot in Relation to 'Adam Bede' Giving the Real Life History of the More Prominent Characters* (Francis Griffiths, 1905)

Myers, W., *The Teachings of George Eliot* (Leicester University Press, 1984)

Nadel, I.B., 'George Eliot and her Biographers' in *Haight and van Asdel (1982)

Newton, K.M., *George Eliot: Romantic Humanist* (Macmillan, 1981)

Noble, T.A., *George Eliot's 'Scenes of Clerical Life'* (Yale University Press, 1965)

Paris, B.J., *Experiments in Life: George Eliot's Quest for Values* (Wayne State University Press, 1965)

Pinney, T. (ed.), *The Essays of George Eliot* (Routledge and Kegan Paul, 1963)

—— 'The Authority of the Past in George Eliot's Novels', *Nineteenth-Century Fiction* 21 (1966), pp. 131-47

Pratt, J.C. and Neufeld, V.A. (eds), *George Eliot's 'Middlemarch' Notebooks: A Transcription* (University of California Press, 1979)

Redinger, R., *George Eliot: The Emergent Self* (Bodley Head, 1975)

Roberts, N., *George Eliot: Her Beliefs and Her Art* (Elek Brooks, 1975)

Robinson, C., '*Romola*: A Reading of the Novel', *Victorian Studies* 6 (1962), pp. 29-42

—— 'The Severe Angel: A Study of *Daniel Deronda*', *English Literary History* 31 (1964), pp. 278-300

Rose, P., *Parallel Lives: Five Victorian Marriages* (Chatto and Windus, 1984)

Scherer, *Essays on English Literature*, trans. by G. Saintsbury (Sampson Low and Company, 1891)

Schorer, M., 'Fiction and the Matrix of Analogy', *Kenyon Review* 11 (1949), pp. 539-60

Showalter, E., *A Literature of their Own: British Women Novelists from Brontë to Lessing* (Princeton University Press, 1977)

Shuttleworth, S., *George Eliot and Nineteenth-Century Science: The Make-Believe of a Beginning* (Cambridge University Press, 1984)

Simcox, E., 'George Eliot', *The Nineteenth Century* 9 (1881), pp. 778-801

—— *Autobiography* [m.s. in Bodleian Library, Oxford]

Smalley, B., *George Eliot and Flaubert: Pioneers of the Modern Novel* (Ohio University Press, 1974)

Smith, A. (ed.), *George Eliot: Centenary Essays and an Unpublished Fragment* (Vision Press, 1980)

Speaight, R., *George Eliot* (Arthur Barker, 1954)

Stang, R. (ed.), *Discussions of George Eliot* (D.C. Heath, 1960) [important essays by Henry James, Barbara Hardy and others]

Stephen, L., *George Eliot* (Macmillan, 1902)

Stump, R., *Movement and Vision in George Eliot's Novels* (University of Washington Press, 1959)

Svaglic, M.J., 'Religion in the Novels of George Eliot', *Journal of English and German Philology* 53 (1954), pp.145-59

Taylor, I., *George Eliot: Woman of Contradictions* (Weidenfeld and Nicolson, 1989)

Thale, J., *The Novels of George Eliot* (Columbia University Press, 1959)

Thomson, F.C., 'The Genesis of *Felix Holt*', *Proceedings of the Modern Language Association* 74 (1959), pp. 576-84

—— '*Felix Holt* as Classic Tragedy', *Nineteenth-Century Fiction* 16 (1961), pp. 47-58

—— 'The Theme of Alienation in *Silas Marner*', *Nineteenth-Century Fiction* 20 (1965), pp. 69-84

Thomson, P., *George Sand and the Victorians: Her Influence in Nineteenth-Century England* (Macmillan, 1977)

Uglow, J., *George Eliot* (Virago, 1987)

Welsh, A., *George Eliot and Blackmail* (Harvard University Press, 1985)

Willey, B., *Nineteenth Century Studies* (Chatto and Windus, 1949)

Williams, B.C., *George Eliot: A Biography* (Macmillan, 1936)

Williams, R., *The English Novel from Dickens to Lawrence* (Chatto and Windus, 1970), pp. 75-94

—— *The Country and the City* (Oxford University Press, 1973), pp. 166-81

Wiesenfarth, J., *A Writer's Notebook, 1854-79, and Uncollected Writings* (University of Virginia Press, 1981)

—— *George Eliot's Mythmaking* (Carl Winter, 1977)

Witemeyer, H., 'English and Italian Portraiture in *Daniel Deronda*', *Nineteenth-Century Fiction* 30 (1976), pp. 477-94

—— *George Eliot and the Visual Arts* (Yale University Press, 1979)

Woolf, V., 'George Eliot', in *The Common Reader* (Hogarth Press, 1932), pp. 166-76

Index

This is deliberately brief, and is divided as follows:

(i) George Eliot's works, main references. References to her translations of Strauss and Feuerbach are given in (ii).
(ii) Selected general index.

Heine, 43, 48, 82, 84
Riehl, 31, 34, 82, 84, 95
'Silly Novels by Lady Novelists', 21, 43, 84, 92
Sterling, 18, 83
Young, 31, 34, 82, 84

Poetry

'Armgart', 29
'Brother and Sister', 28, 32, 81, 87
'The Choir Invisible', 32
'Self and Life', 87
The Spanish Gypsy, 11, 21-2, 29, 45-6, 49, 100

Selected Index

Acton, J., 16-17, 24, 62
Adams, K., 105
Ashton, R., 99-100, 105
Axon, W.E.A., 23-4
Beaty, J., 75-7
Beer, G., 90-1, 100-1
Bennett, A., 26
Bennett, J., 58-60
Blackwood, J., 5, 14, 63
Blind, M., 21-2, 80, 86
Bodichon, B., 63, 92
Bonaparte, F., 99
Bourl'honne, P., 52
Bray, Cara, 48, 63, 79, 103
Bray, Charles, 51, 63, 103
Brownell, W.C., 25-6
Browning, O., 22-3
Bullett, G., 52-3
Cecil, D., 36-42
Chapman, J., 45-6, 51-2, 61-3
Clarke, C. (GE's sister), 79
Colvin, S., 13
Comte, A., 46, 48, 62, 80, 93, 96, 102
Congreve, Mrs, 64, 80
Cross, J.W., 1, 16, 18-21, 32, 61-4, 76, 78, 82, 86, 88-9
Cunningham, V., 95-6
Dallas, E.S., 6, 8
Darwin, C., 100-1